Copyright © 2019 by A.J. Olvera • All original artwork by JP farquar

Graphic Design by Aída Ramírez • nidelviaaida@me.com • portfolio: https://aidafotografia.pixieset.com//diseo/

All rights reserved. No part of this publication may be reproduced, distributed, or transmitted in any form or by any means, including photocopying, recording, or other electronic or mechanical methods, without the prior written permission of the publisher, except in the case of brief quotations embodied in critical reviews and certain other noncommercial uses permitted by copyright law. For permission requests, write to the publisher, addressed "Attention: Permissions Coordinator."

Printed in the United States of America

First Printing, 2019

ISBN: 978-057856-914-7

You Might Be a Psychedelic Chaosatanist If....

For the Beast and Babalon

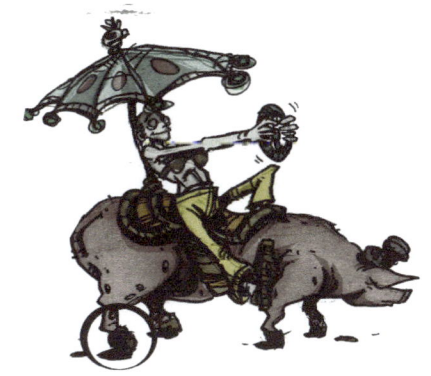

You Might Be a Psychedelic Chaosatanist If....

You've had a profound, spiritual or cathartic experience on psychedelic drugs.

Burn in hell!
God hates what you like!
BIGGUNS

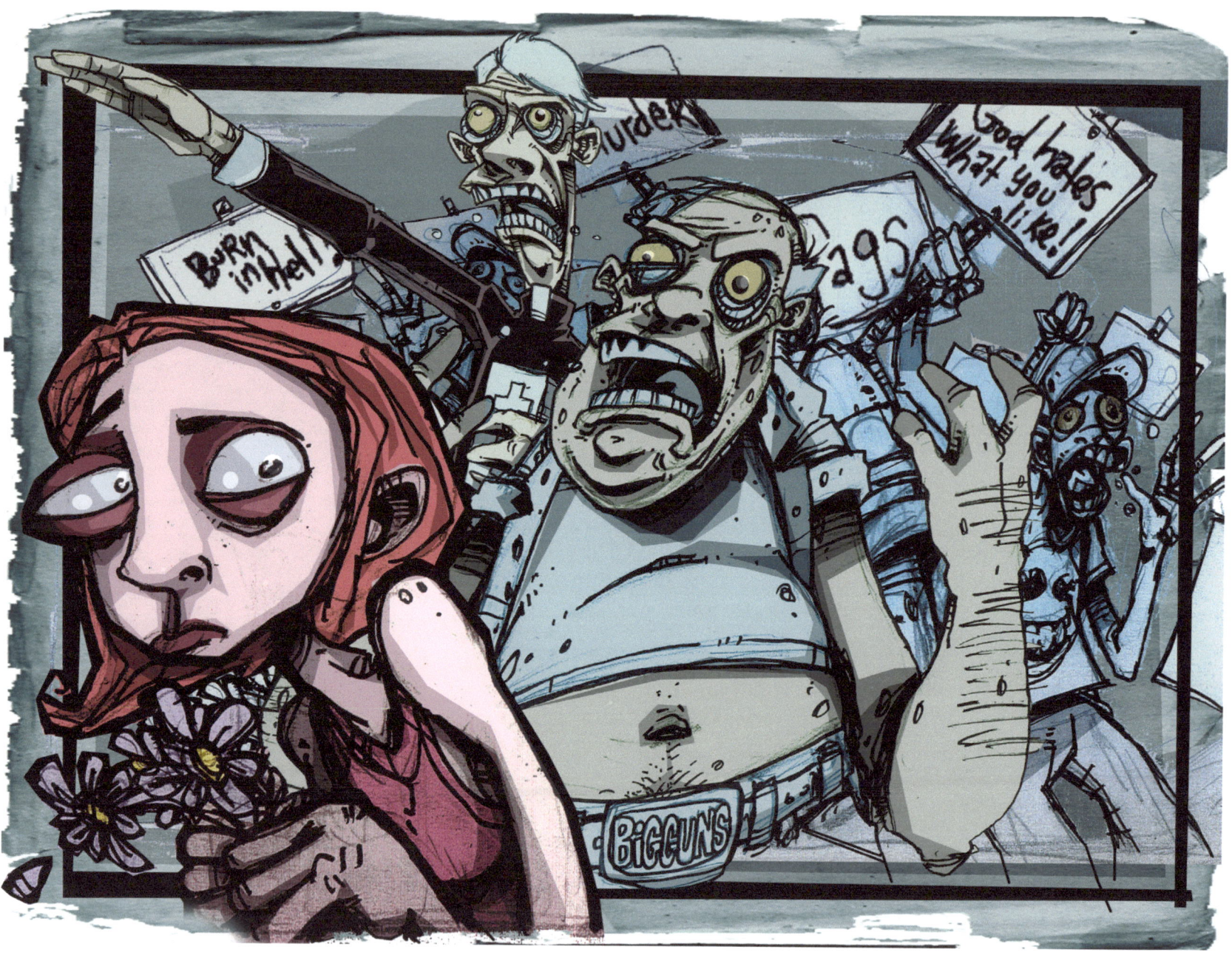

You Might Be a Psychedelic Chaosatanist If....

You find religious dogma distasteful.

You Might Be a Psychedelic Chaosatanist If....

You're attracted to the bad boys instead of the nice guys.

Le Dinehaus(2)
Puh.

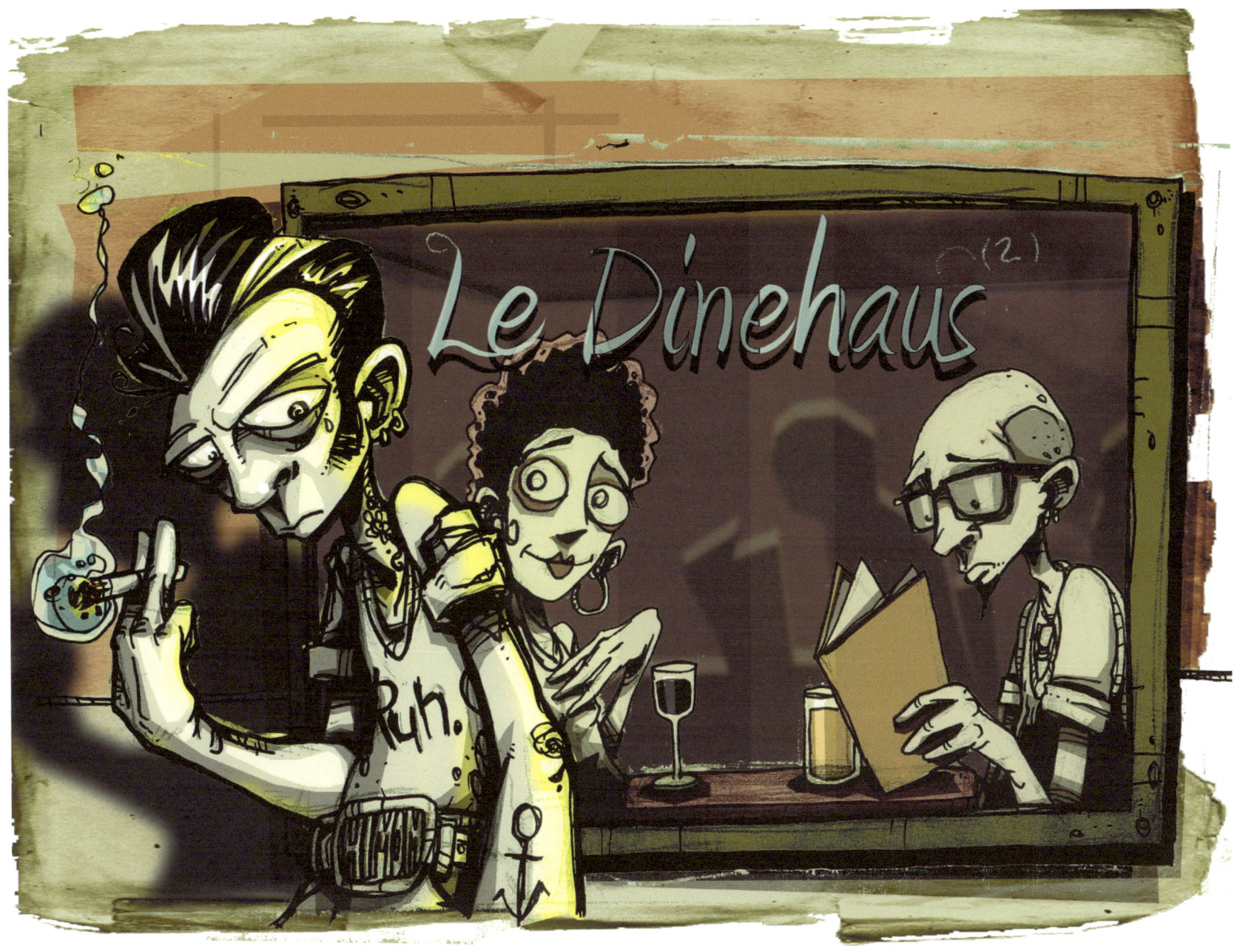

You Might Be a Psychedelic Chaosatanist If....

You think that intelligence is sexy

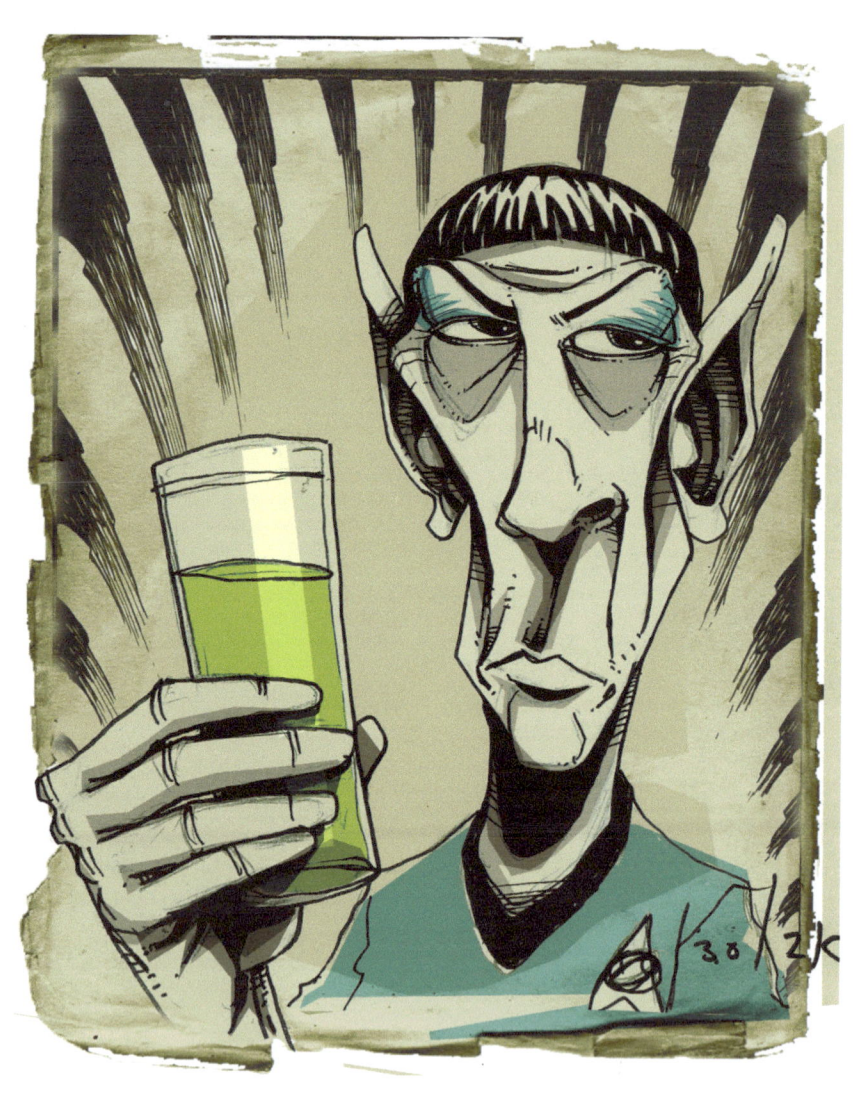

You Might Be a Psychedelic Chaosatanist If....

You secretly root for the bad guy.

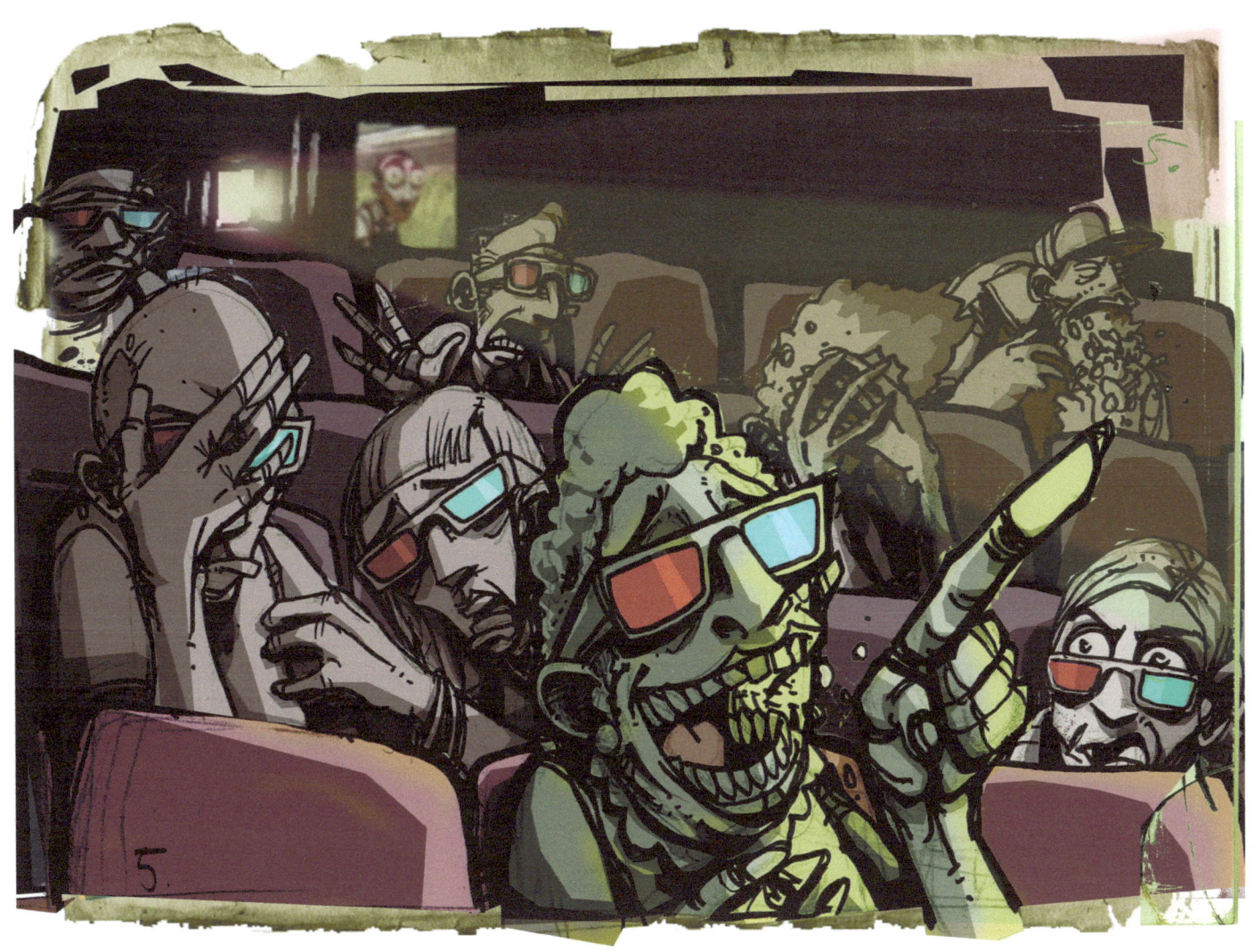

You Might Be a Psychedelic Chaosatanist If....

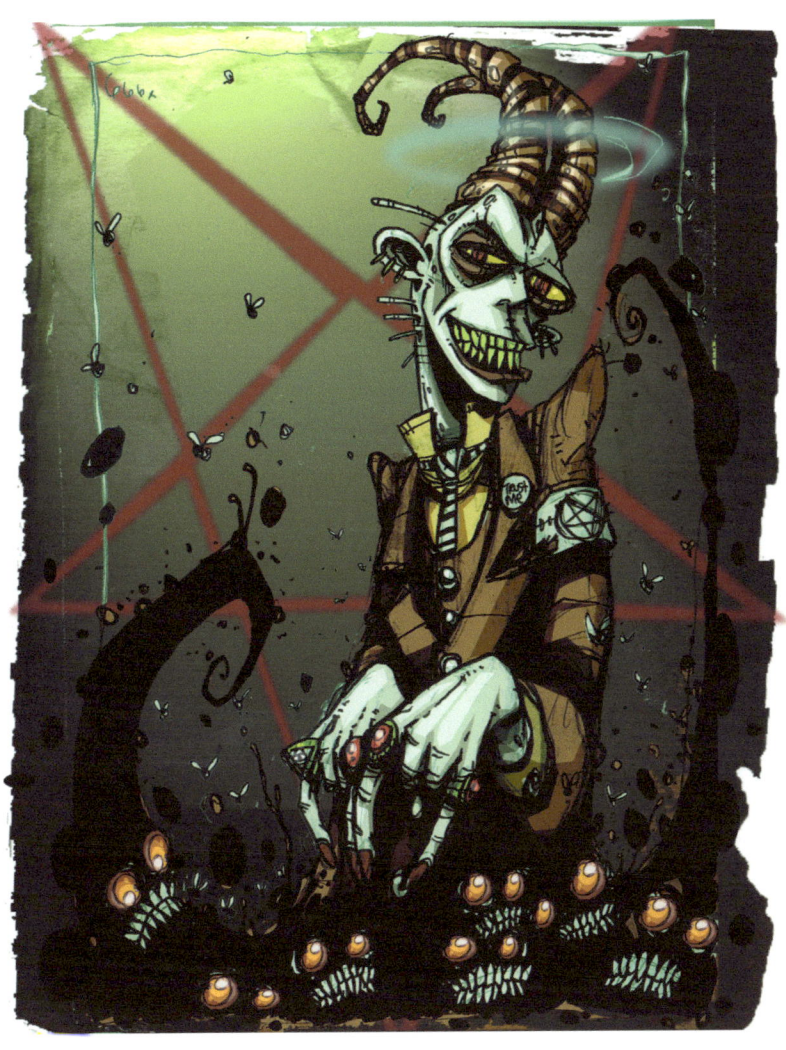

You think the devil is a charming man...

Or a tempting woman.

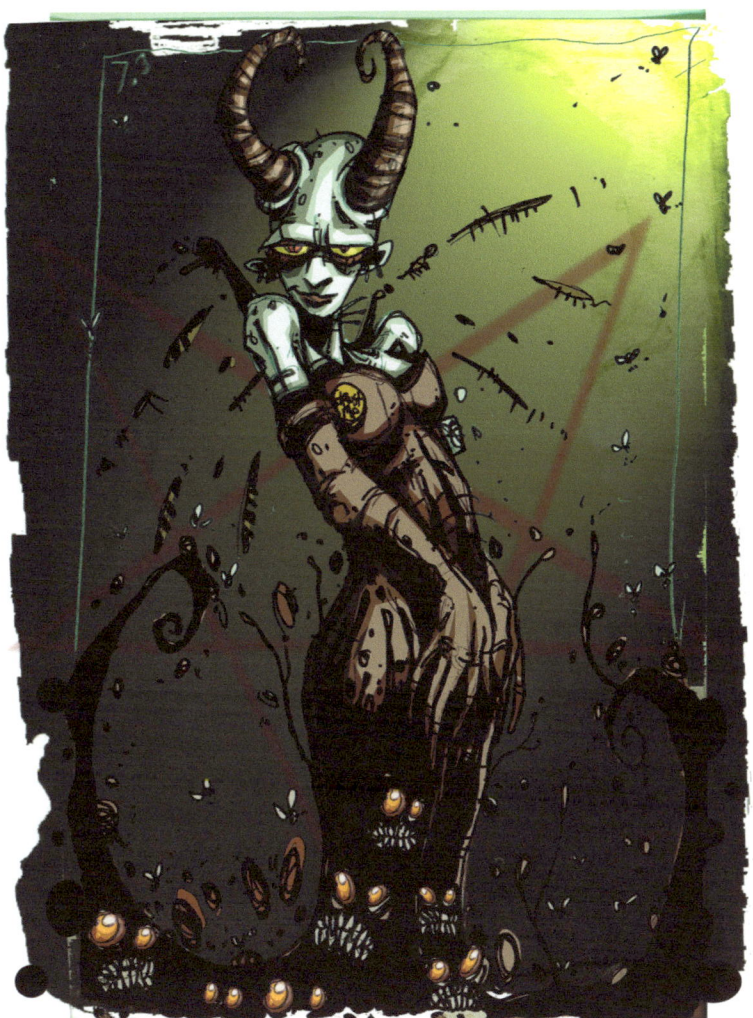

YOU MIGHT BE A PSYCHEDELIC CHAOSATANIST IF....

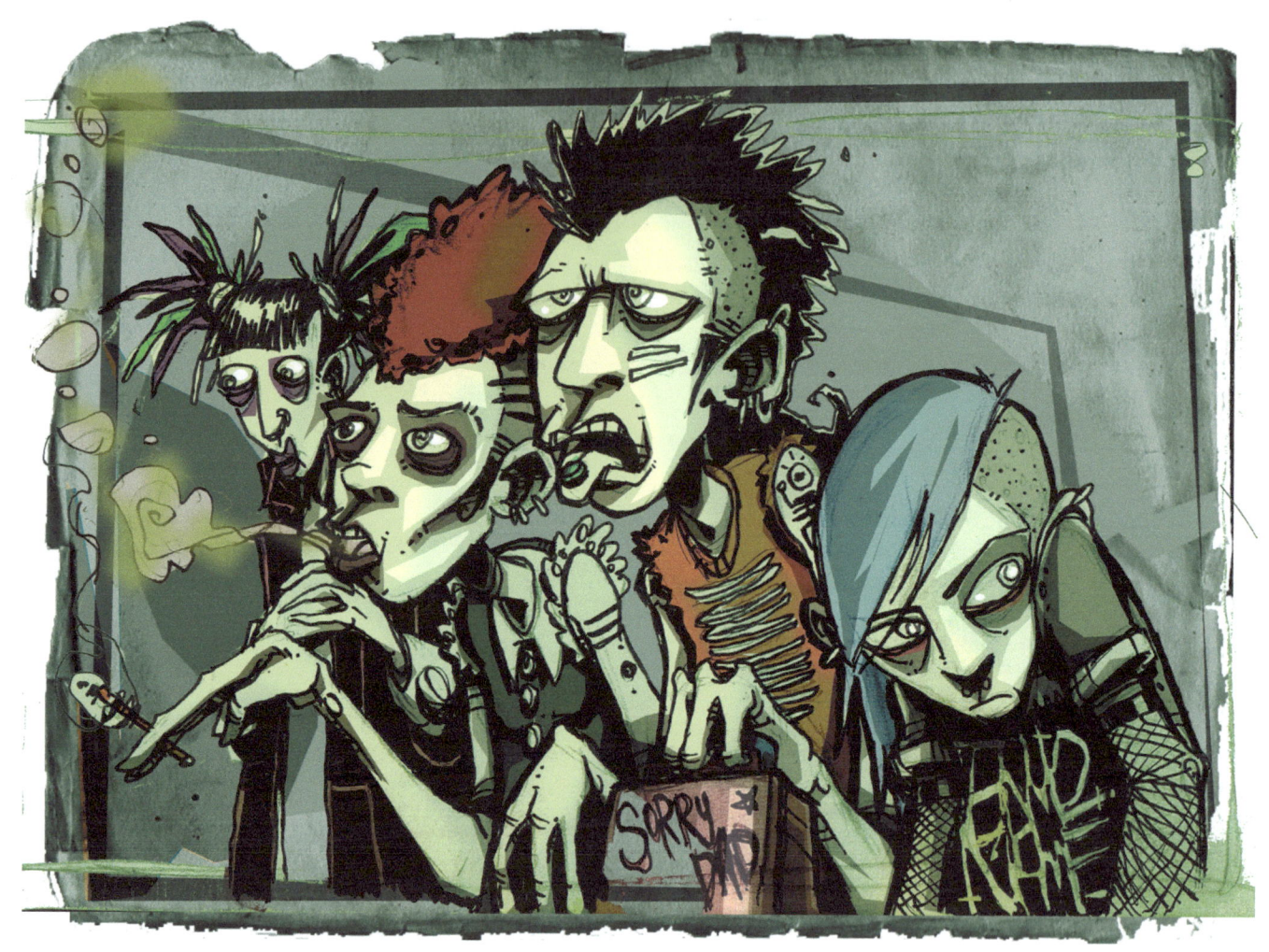

You are into Fandom, Cosplay, BDSM, Goth-Industrial subculture AND you like psychedelics.

You Might Be a Psychedelic Chaosatanist If....

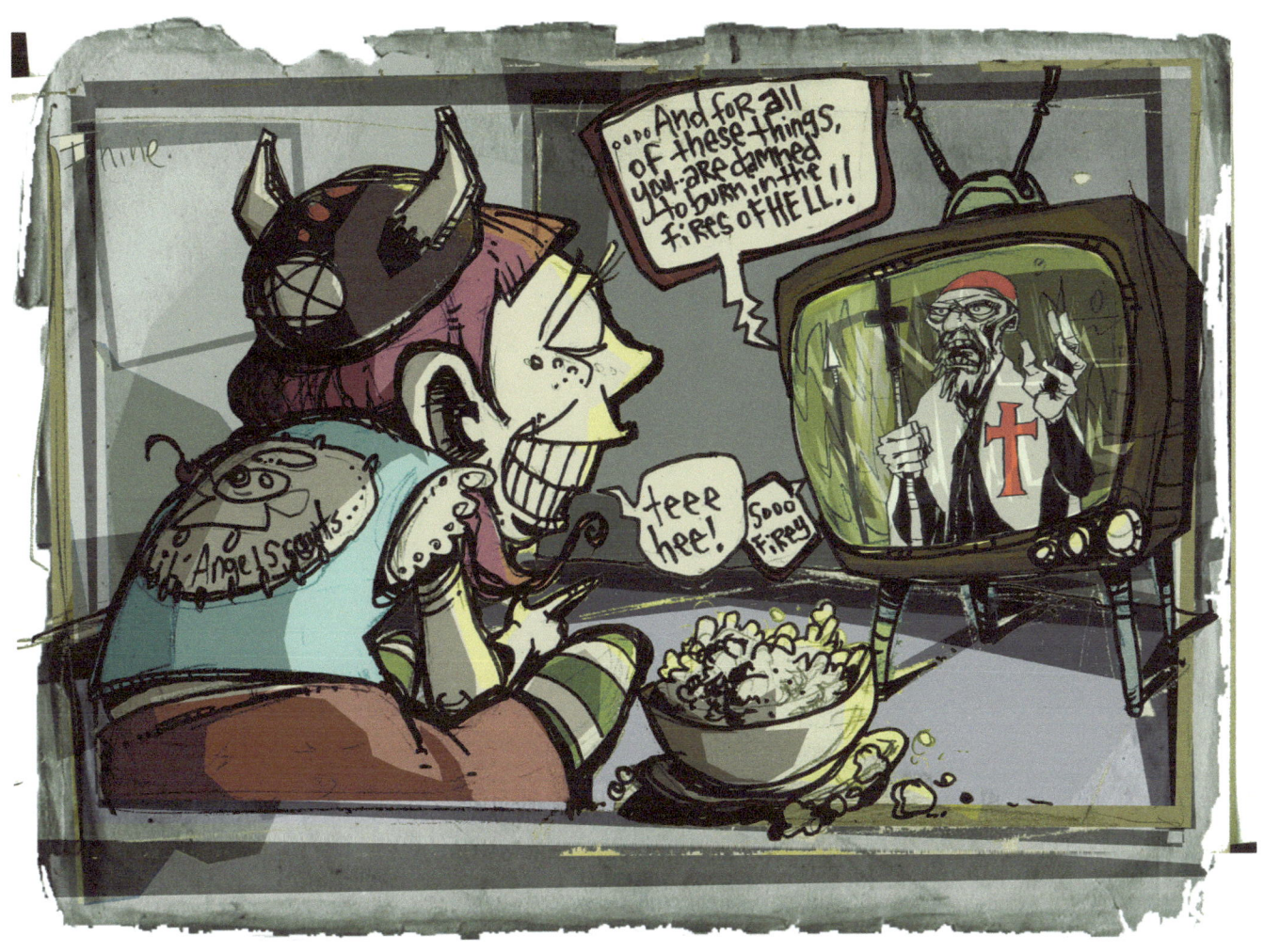

You think religious horror flicks are comedy.

You Might Be a Psychedelic Chaosatanist If....

You aren't afraid of the dark.

You Might Be a Psychedelic Chaosatanist If....

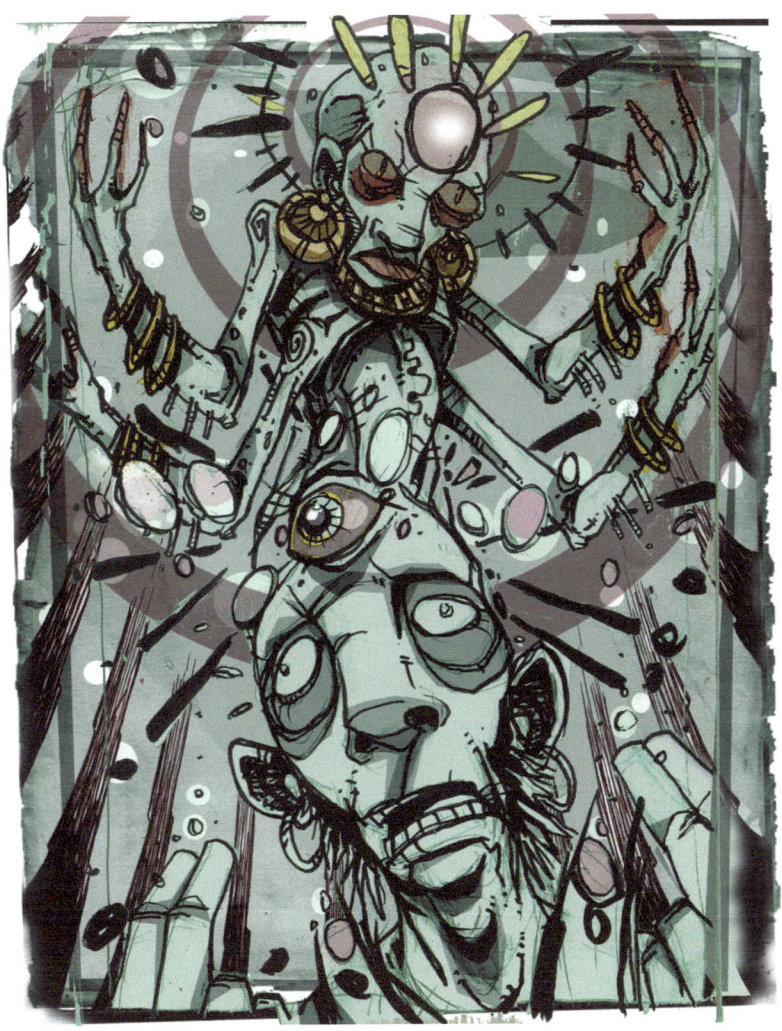

You've ever thought that you were a god.
(Extra points if you were tripping.)

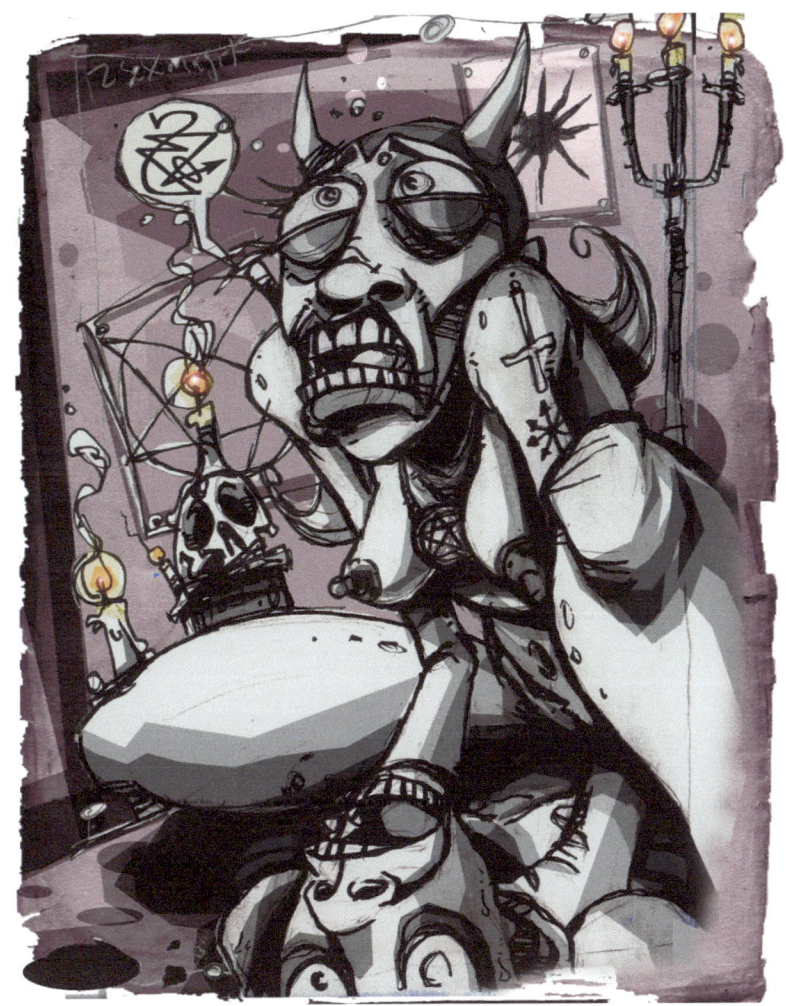

You like Sex Magick.

You Might Be a Psychedelic Chaosatanist If....

You've ever been part of someone's homemade pagan ritual.

moon ritual

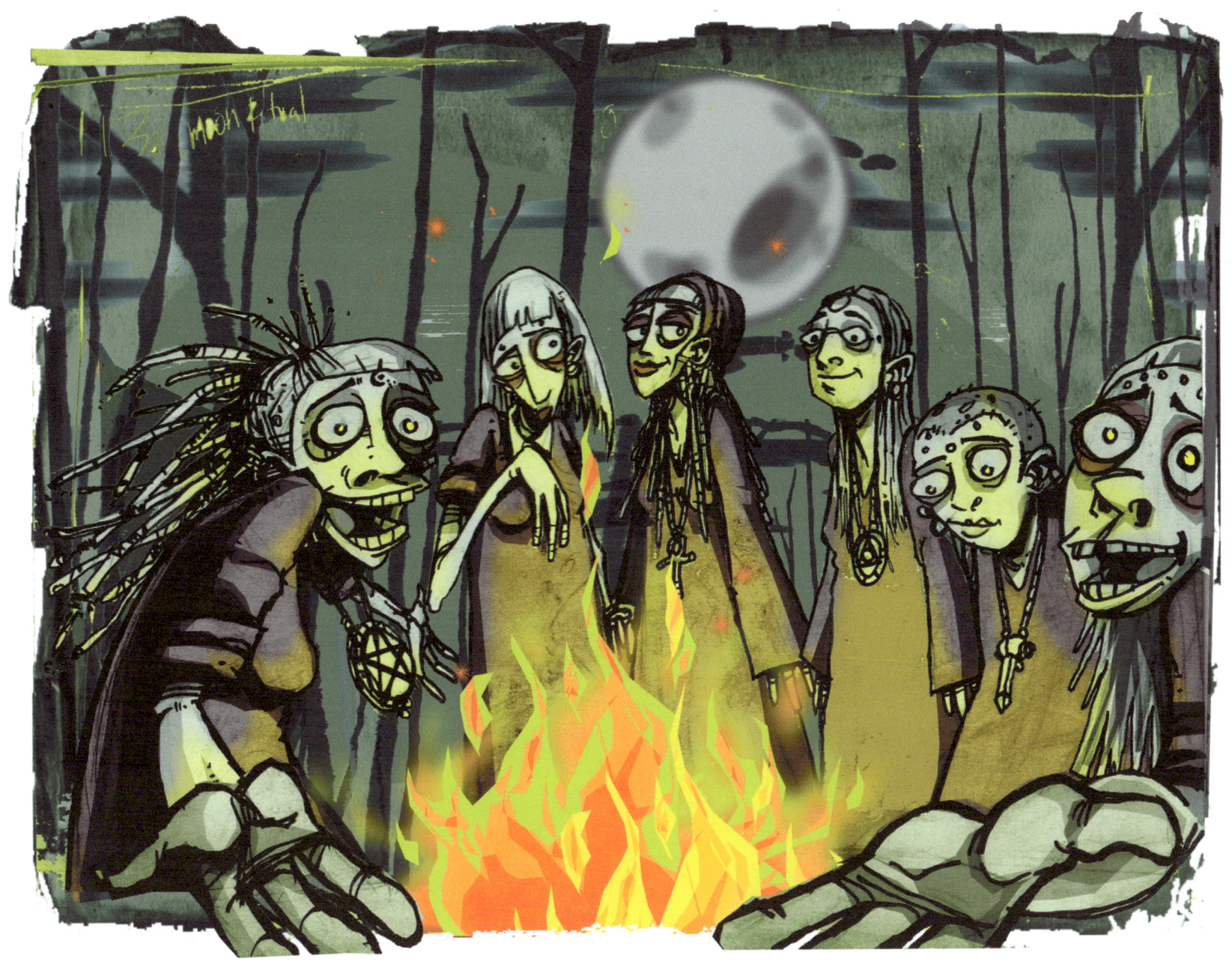

YOU MIGHT BE A PSYCHEDELIC CHAOSATANIST IF....

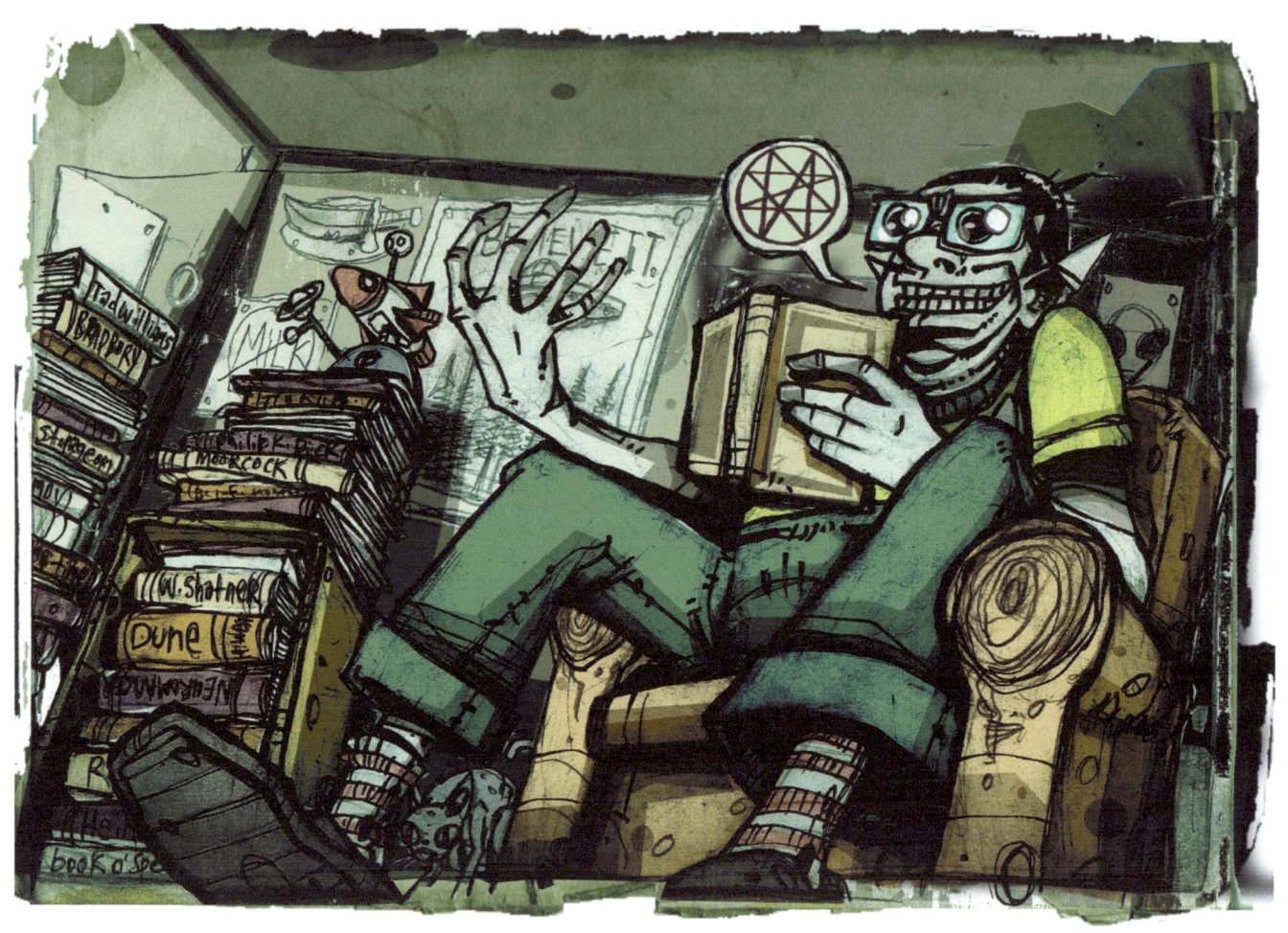

You derive more inspiration from reading science fiction or fantasy than you do from reading holy texts.

You Might Be a Psychedelic Chaosatanist If....

You enjoy sex free of guilt or judgment.

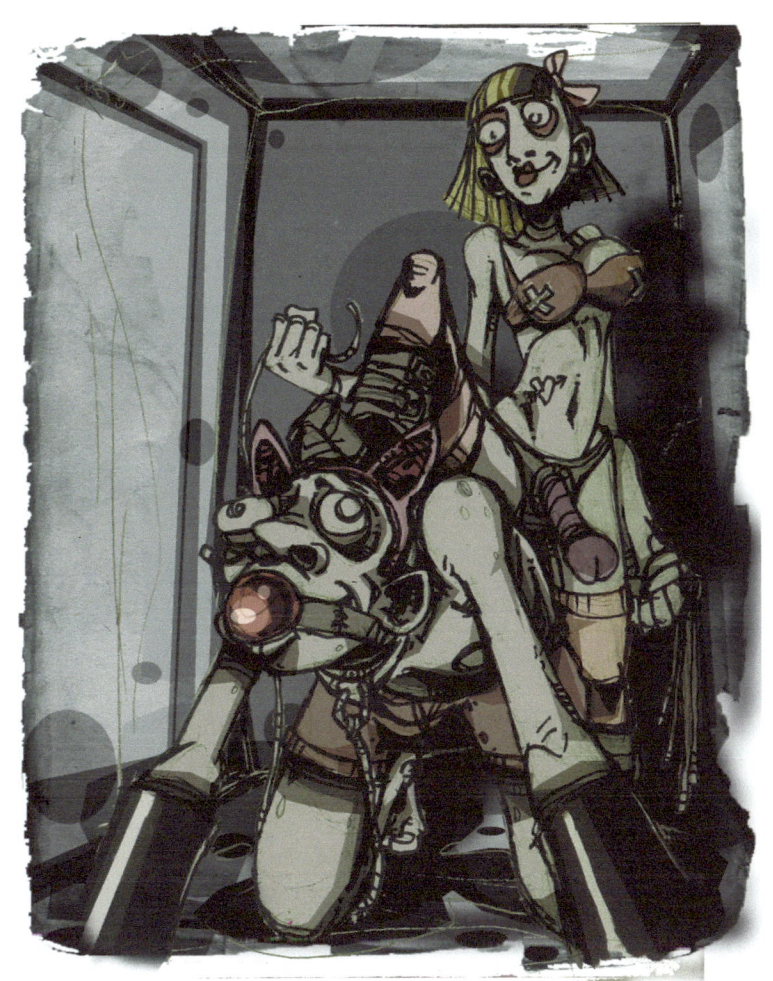

Chaos Magick hall of fame
AUSTIN OSMAN SPARE
ALEISTER CROWLEY
PETER CARROLL
JHONN BALANCE
GENESIS P ORRIDGE
ROBERT ANTON WILSON

You Might Be a Psychedelic Chaosatanist If....

You know who some of these people are.

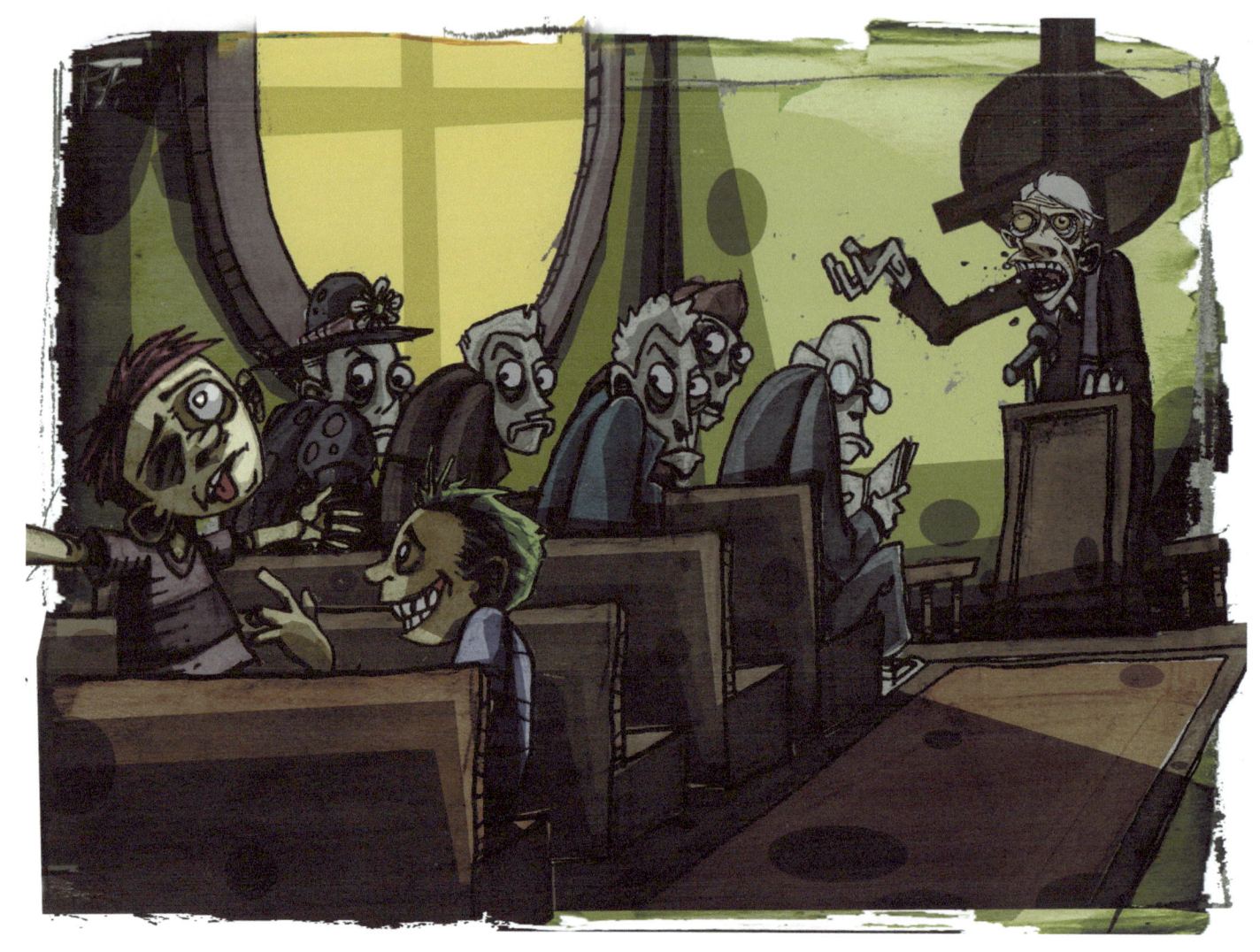

You Might Be a Psychedelic Chaosatanist If....

You have ever made fun of religion.

You Might Be a Psychedelic Chaosatanist If....

You have been to Burning Man, or any other drug-fueled, clothing-optional, large-scale, pagan festival.

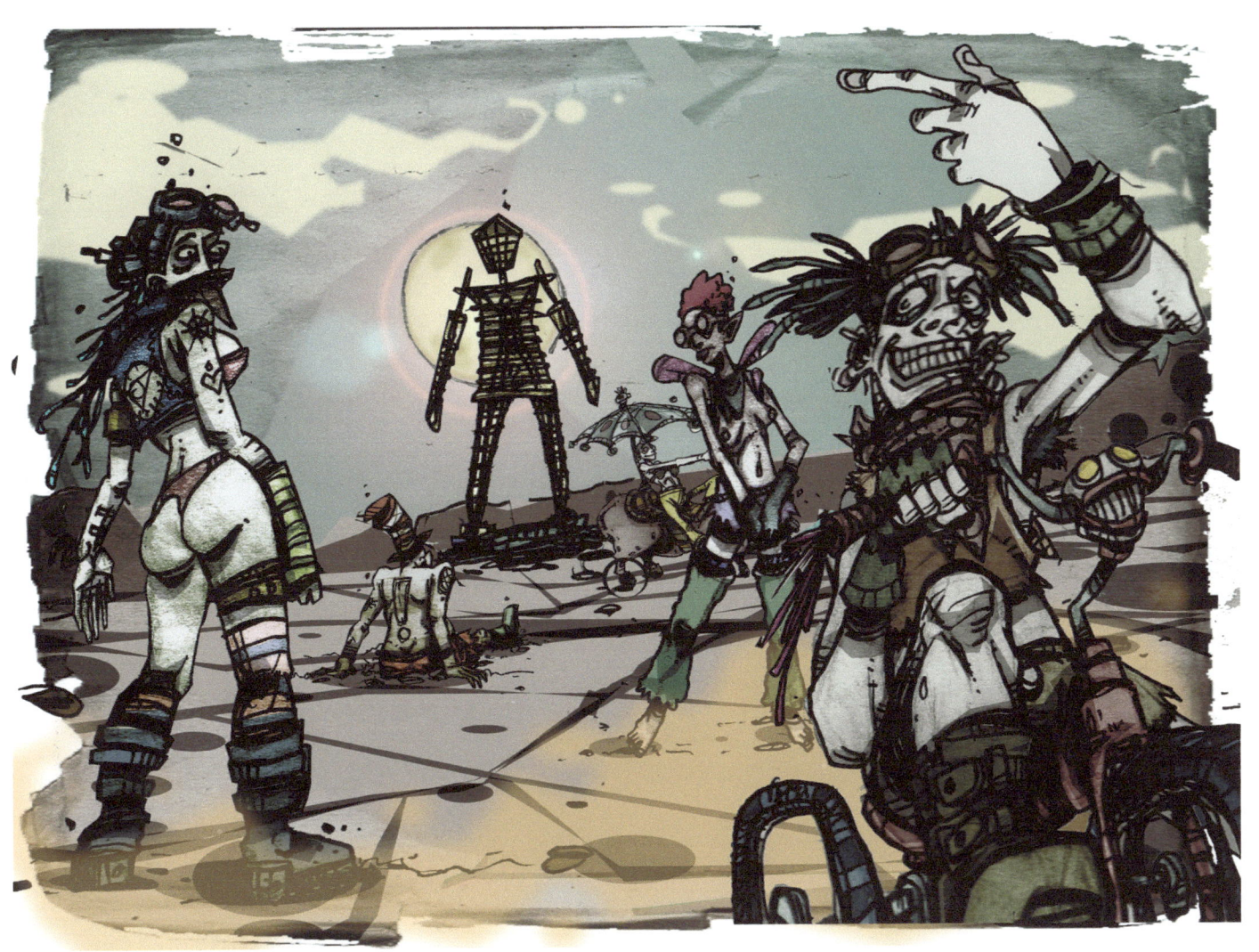

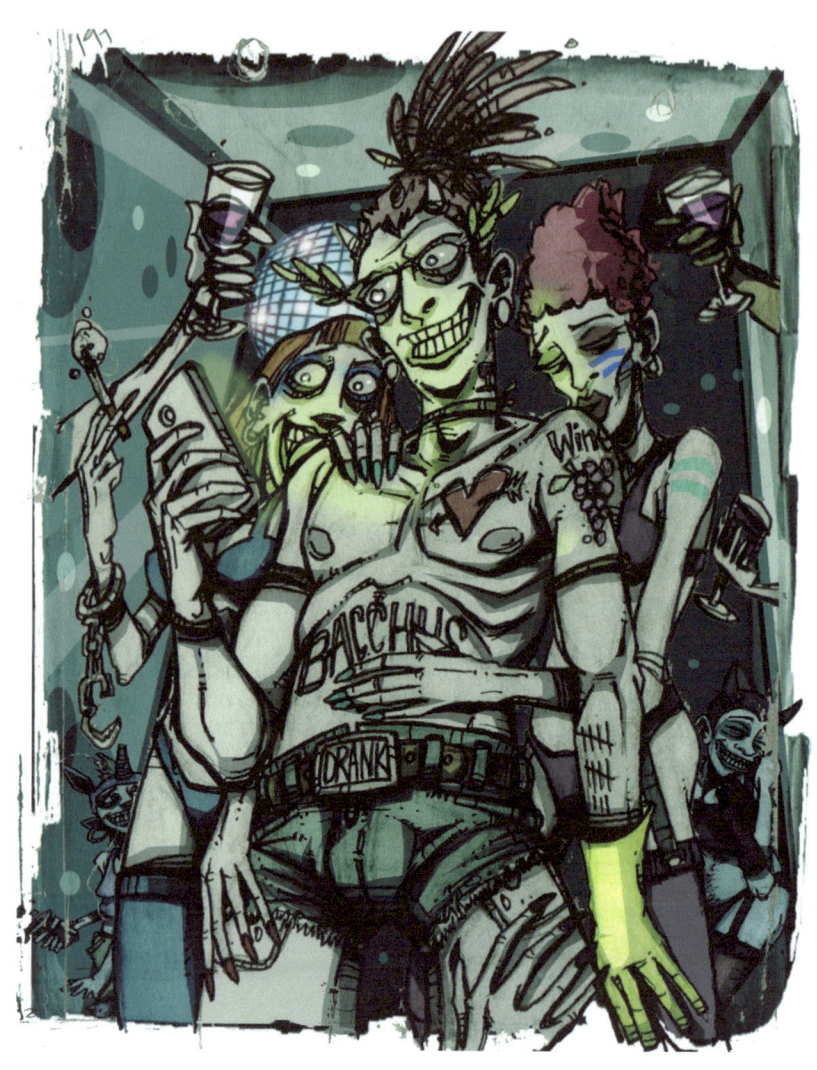

You Might Be a Psychedelic Chaosatanist If....

You've traded ignorant bliss for bacchanalian realism.

You Might Be a Psychedelic Chaosatanist If....

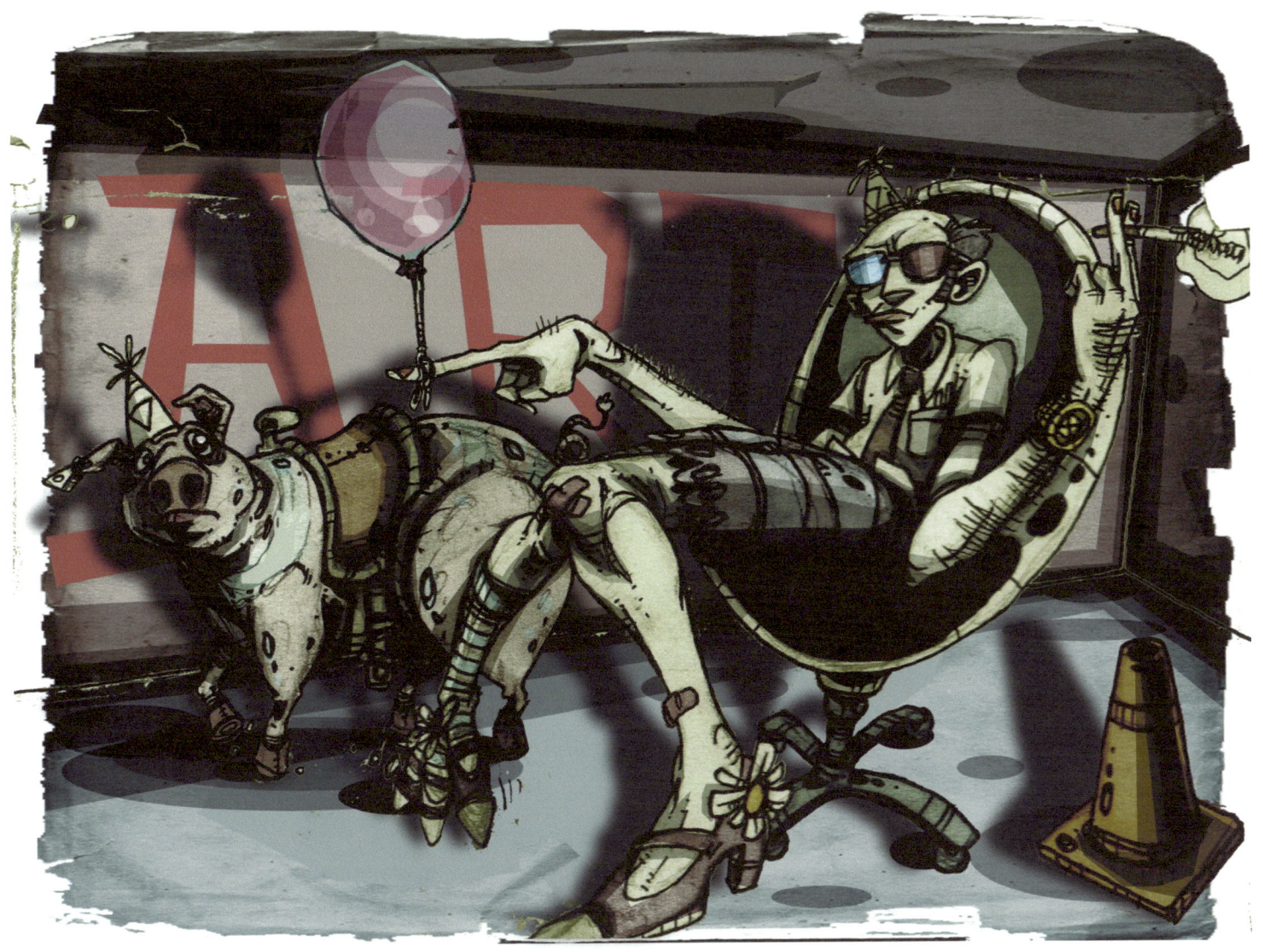

You don't care what people think of you.

You Might Be a Psychedelic Chaosatanist If....

You have ever worn a devil costume for fun.

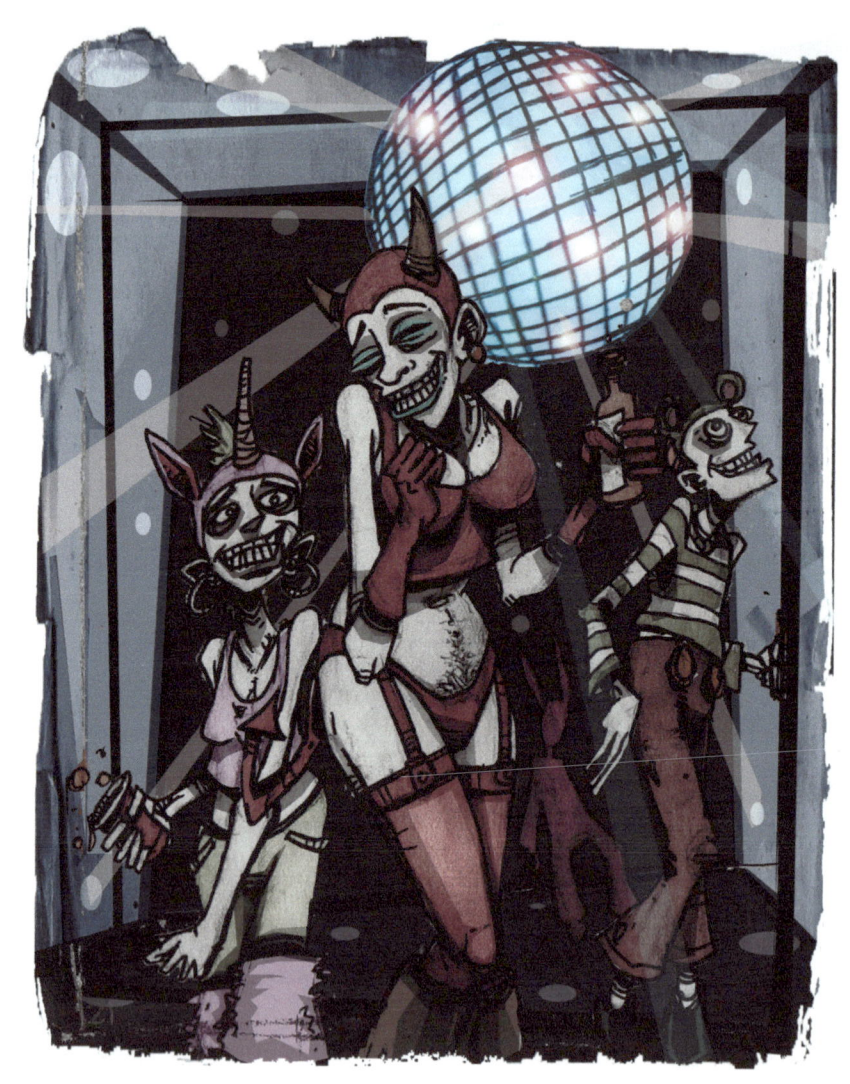

You Might Be a Psychedelic Chaosatanist If....

You sometimes love the air, trees, water and animals more than other humans.

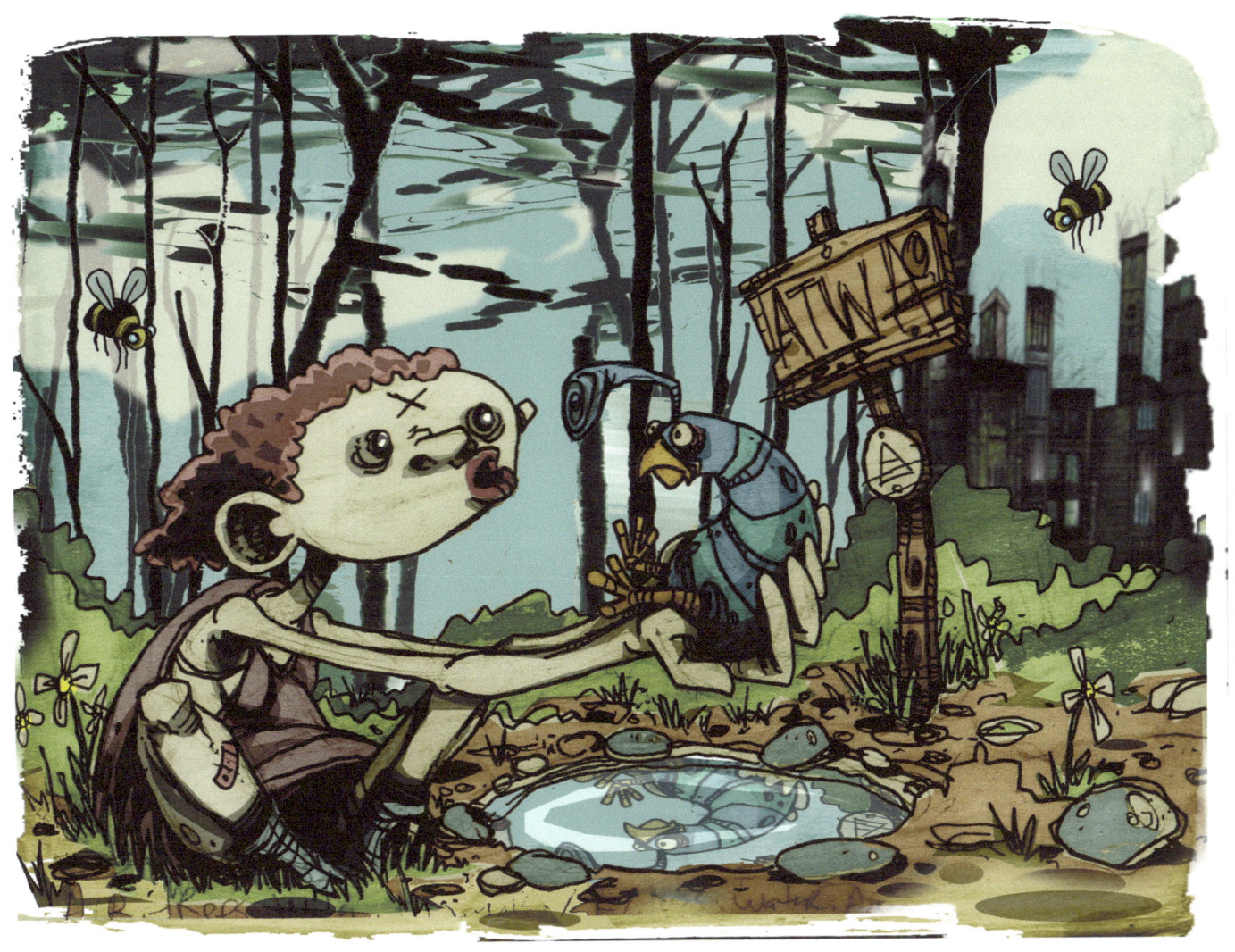

You Might Be a Psychedelic Chaosatanist If....

You are more interested in the "here and now" than in the alleged "hereafter".

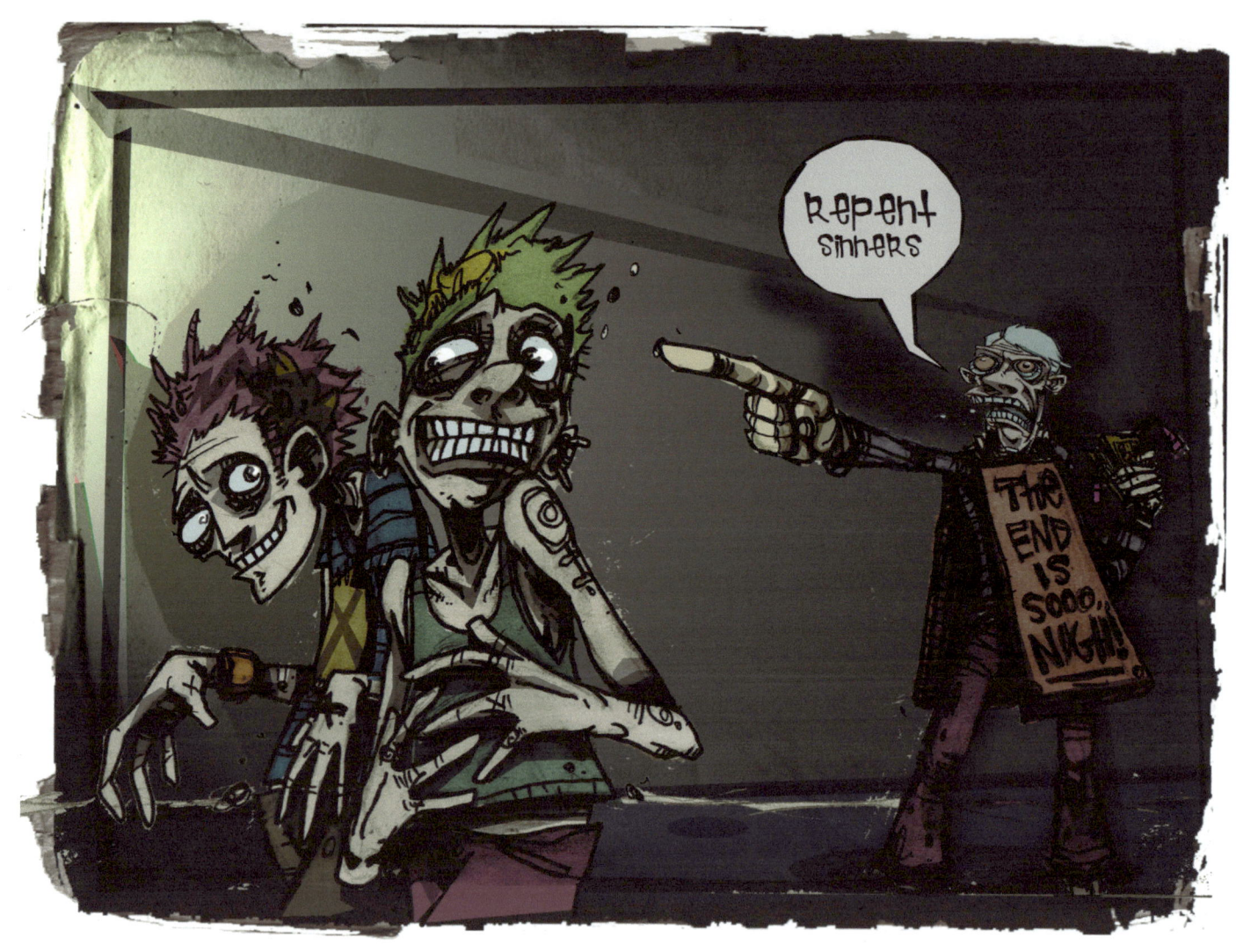

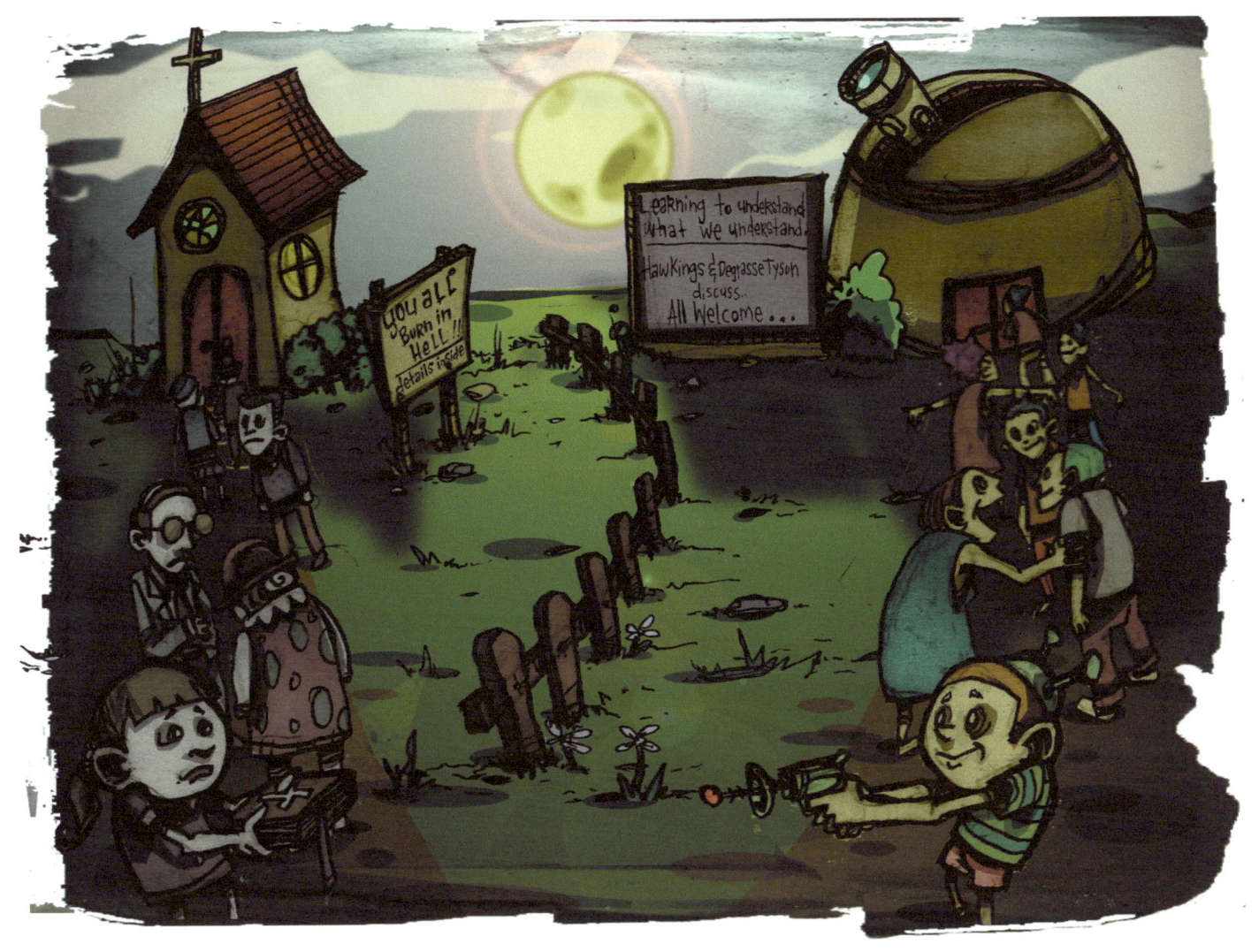

You Might Be a Psychedelic Chaosatanist If....

If you have to choose, you'll choose science.

You Might Be a Psychedelic Chaosatanist If....

You think of religions like works of ancient art: mythical stories that encapsulate cultural vestiges of a distant past.

hang in there.
HOLY BIBLE
GRIMMS
Seuss
illyiad • homer

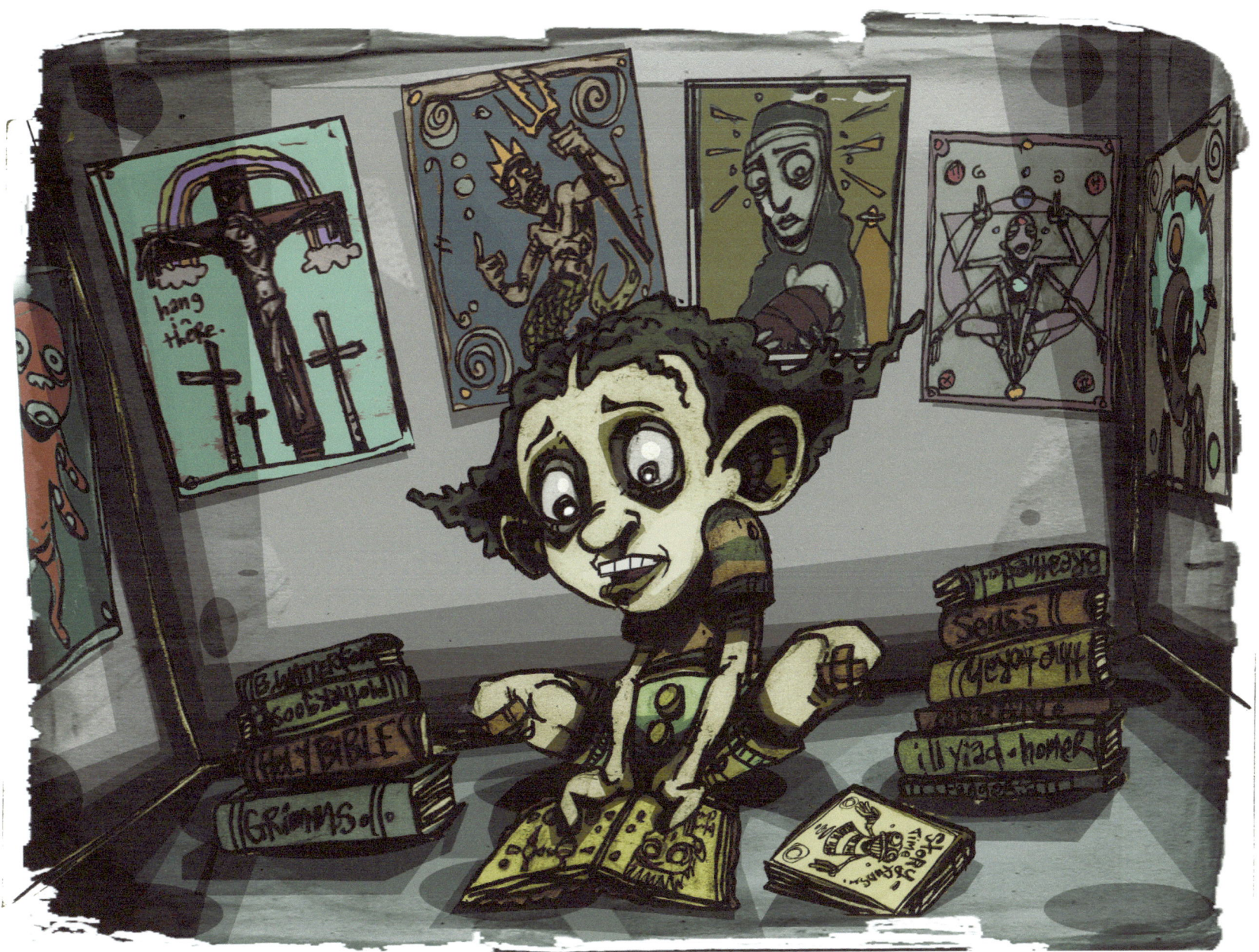

You Might Be a Psychedelic Chaosatanist If....

You have engaged in anti-authoritarian protest behavior.

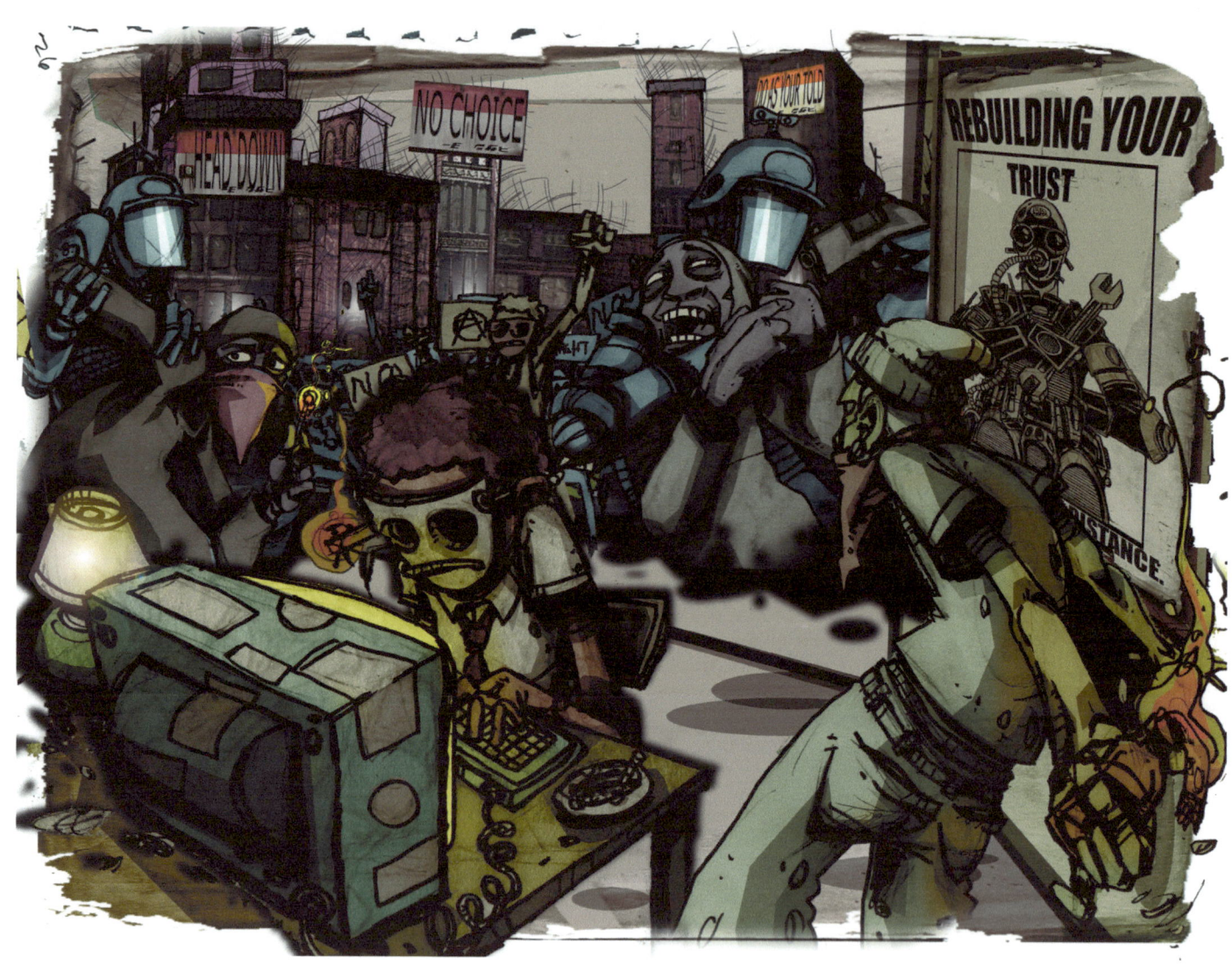

You Might Be a Psychedelic Chaosatanist If....

You have met the Machine Elves.

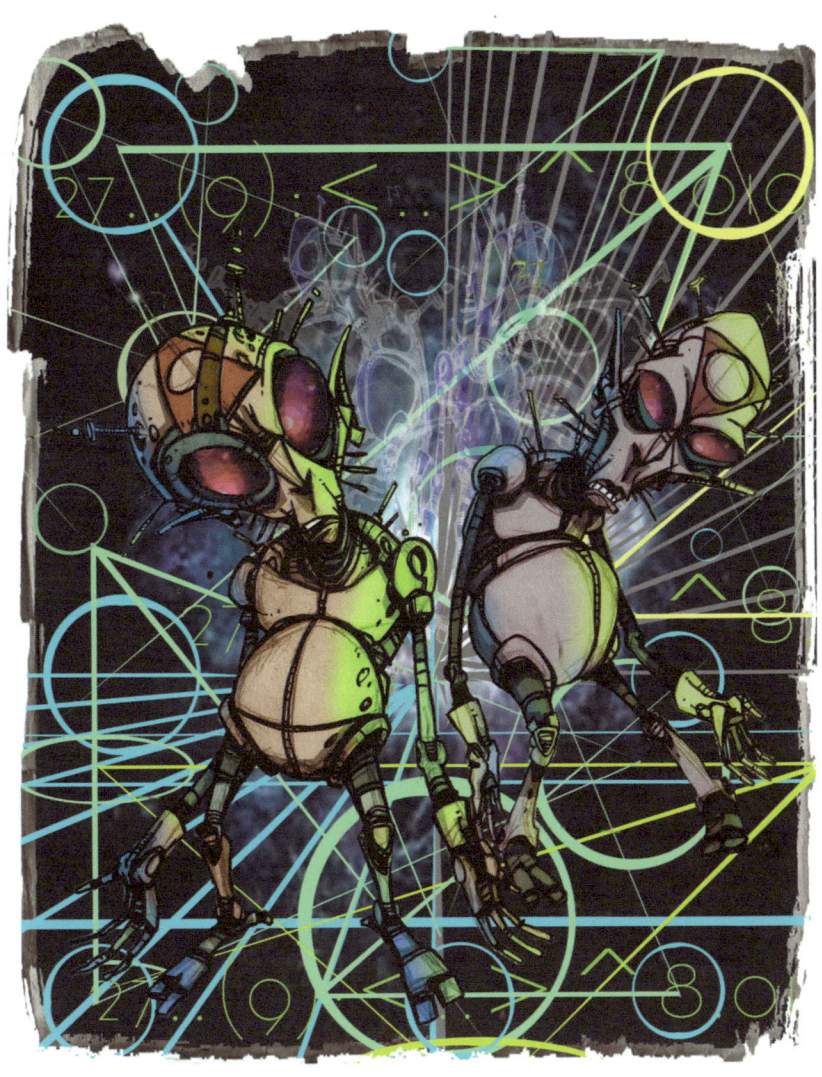

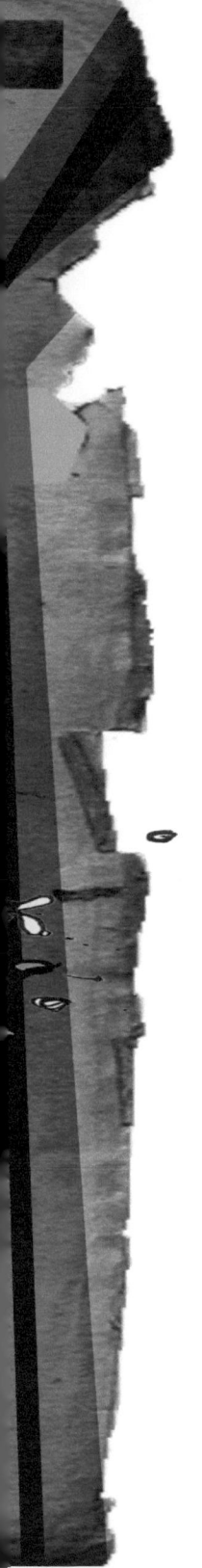

You Might Be a Psychedelic Chaosatanist If....

You think organized religion has failed to such an extent
that its nemesis appears to have a superior moral compass.

YOU MIGHT BE A PSYCHEDELIC CHAOSATANIST IF....

The movie "Altered States" influenced your early drug explorations.

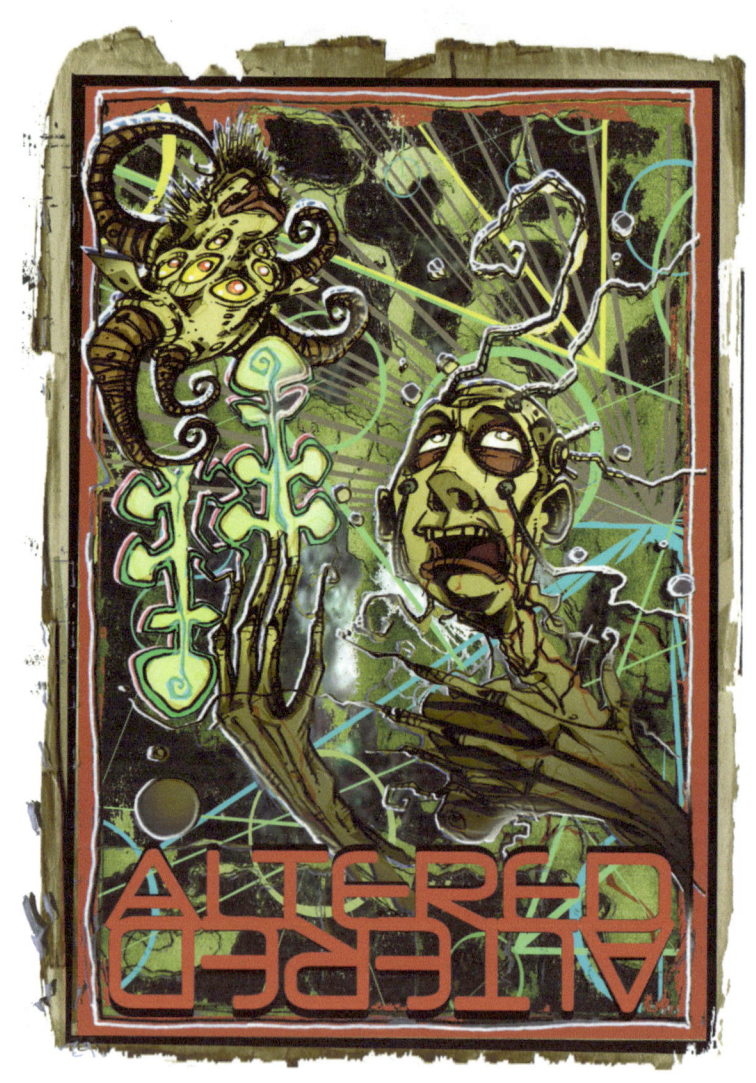

You Might Be a Psychedelic Chaosatanist If....

You like atheists, but you love artists.

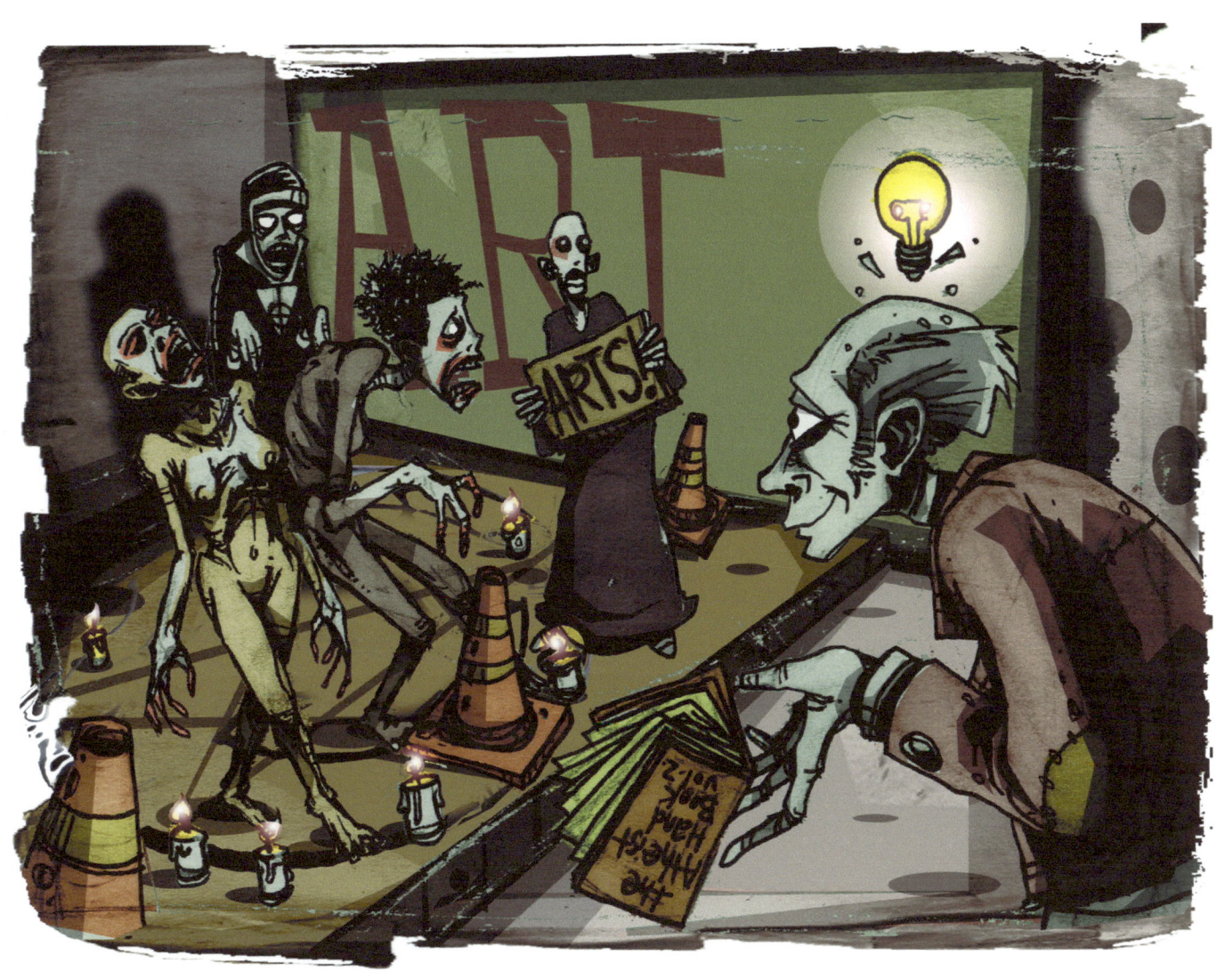

You Might Be a Psychedelic Chaosatanist If....

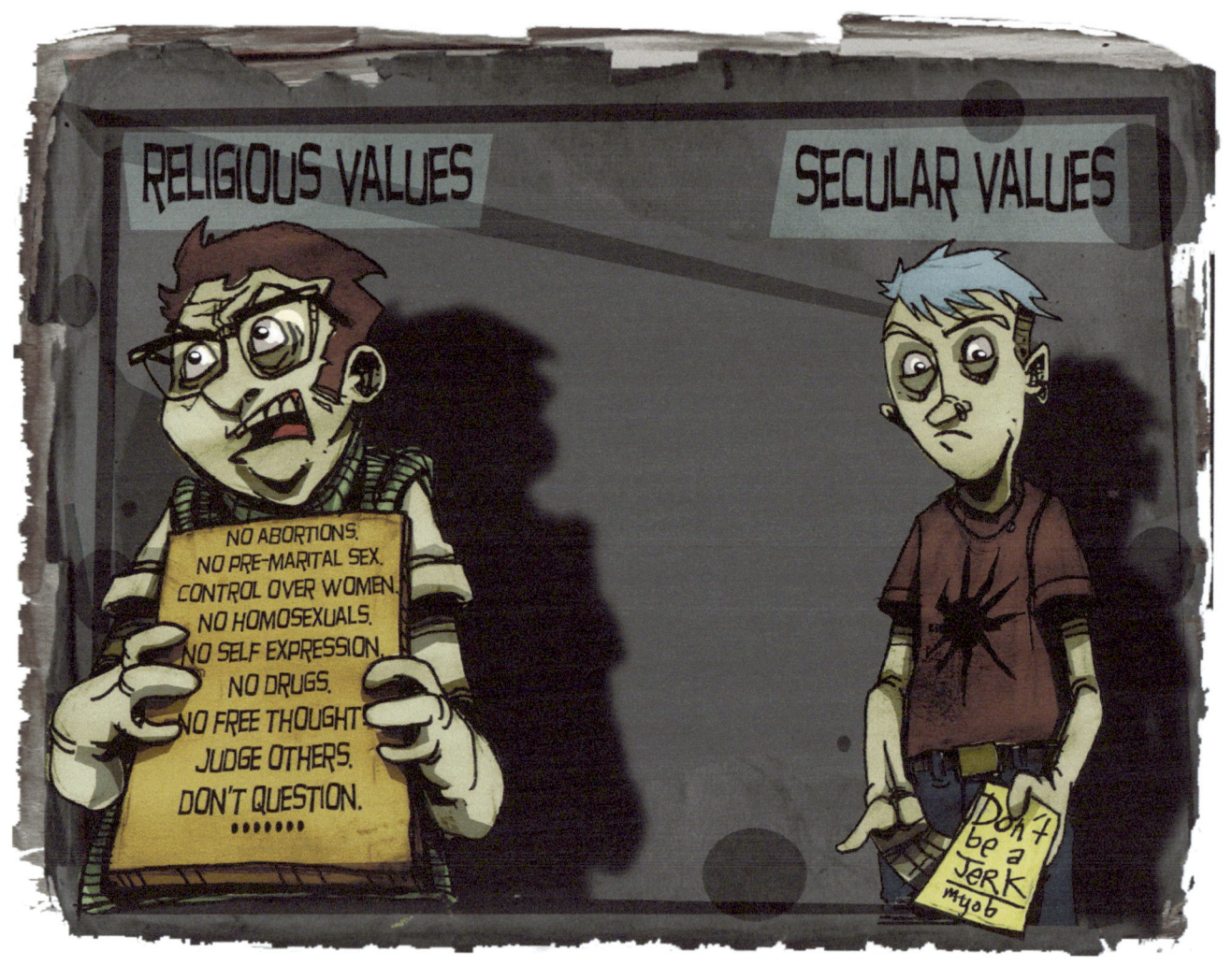

You frequently find yourself with an opinion opposite that of religious folks.

You Might Be a Psychedelic Chaosatanist If....

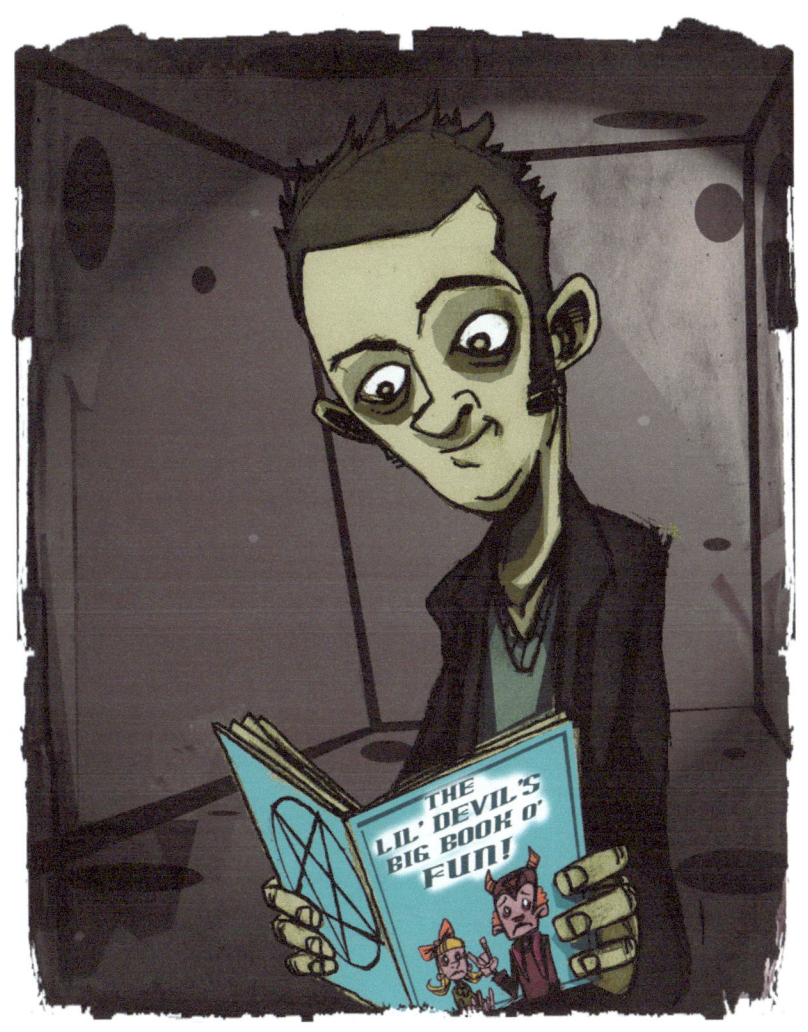

You think that humor is a natural response to the absurdity of religious dogma.

You Might Be a Psychedelic Chaosatanist If....

You can answer, "Yes" to the questions: "Are you Experienced?" and "Did you pass the Acid Test?"

You Might Be a Psychedelic Chaosatanist If….

You are a secular humanist who simply likes satanic iconography and psychedelics.

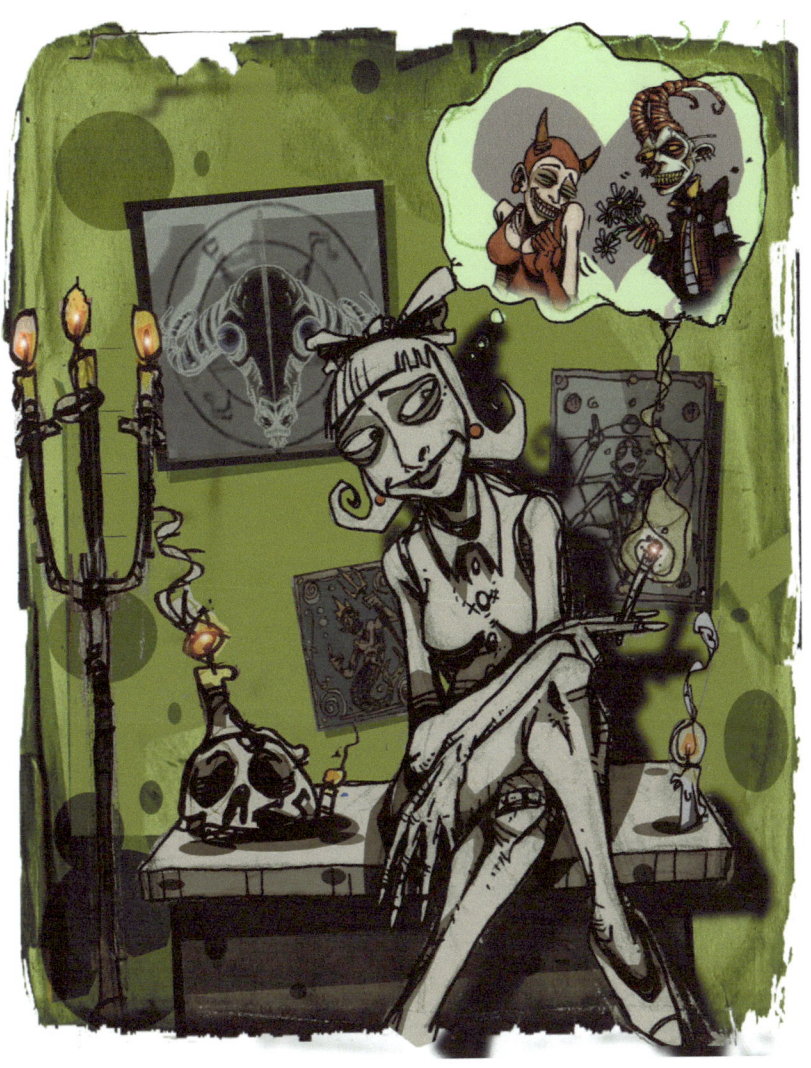

Judaism.
buddhism...
islam
christianity
Catholicism.

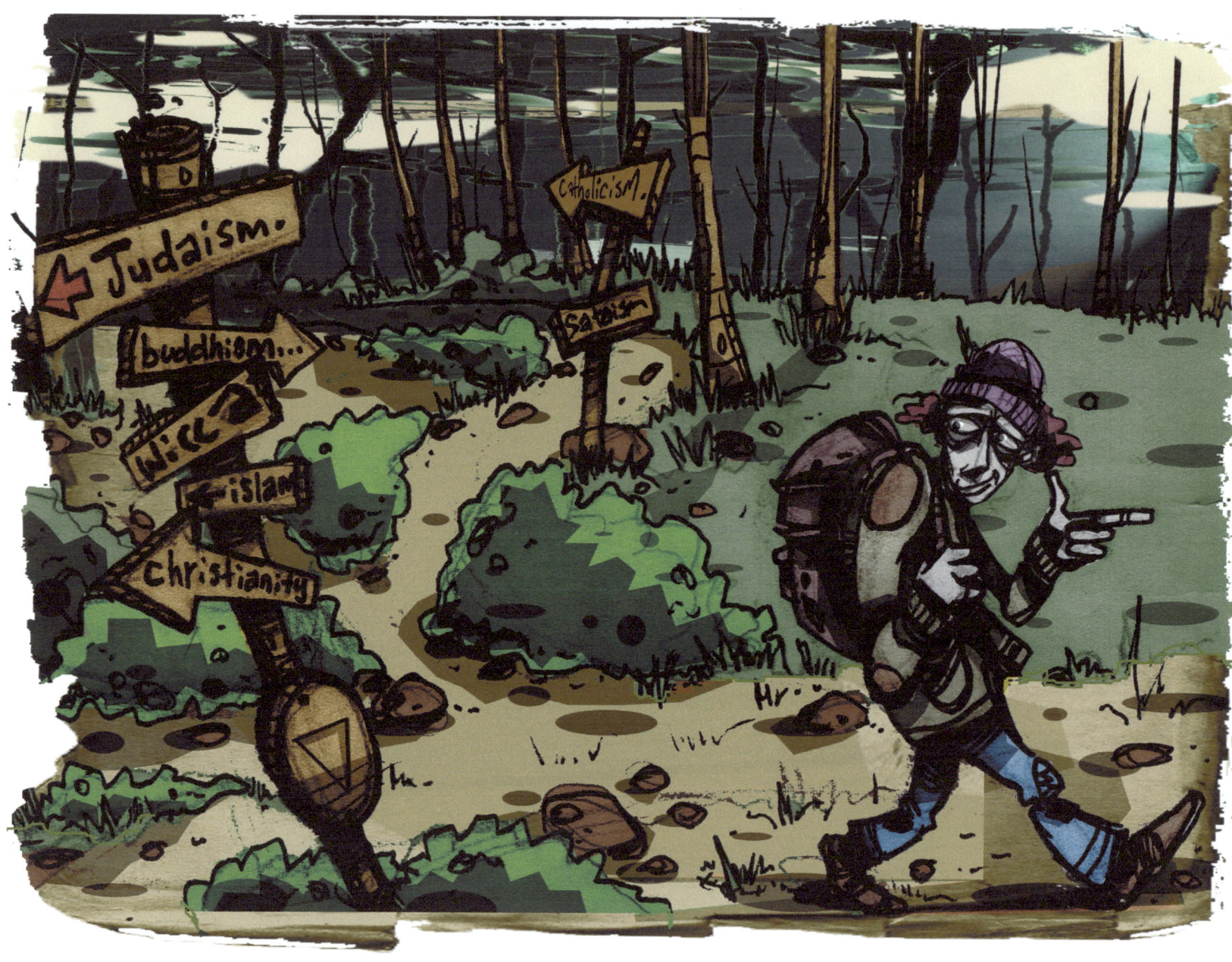

You Might Be a Psychedelic Chaosatanist If....

You find yourself in a religious category of one, defined by your inability to believe religious claims, while still being curious about the possibilities of transcendence.

YOU MIGHT BE A PSYCHEDELIC CHAOSATANIST IF....

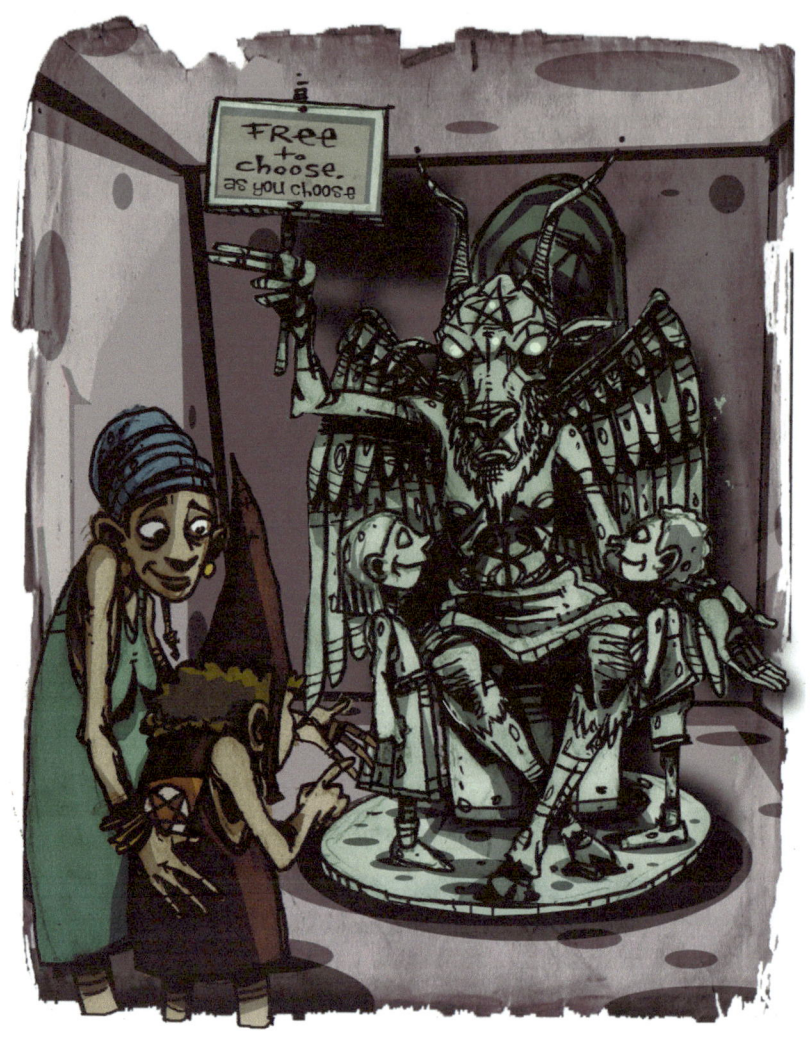

You grasp how the icons of darkness can subvert the dominant paradigm by unmasking those who misuse the icons of light.

You Might Be a Psychedelic Chaosatanist If....

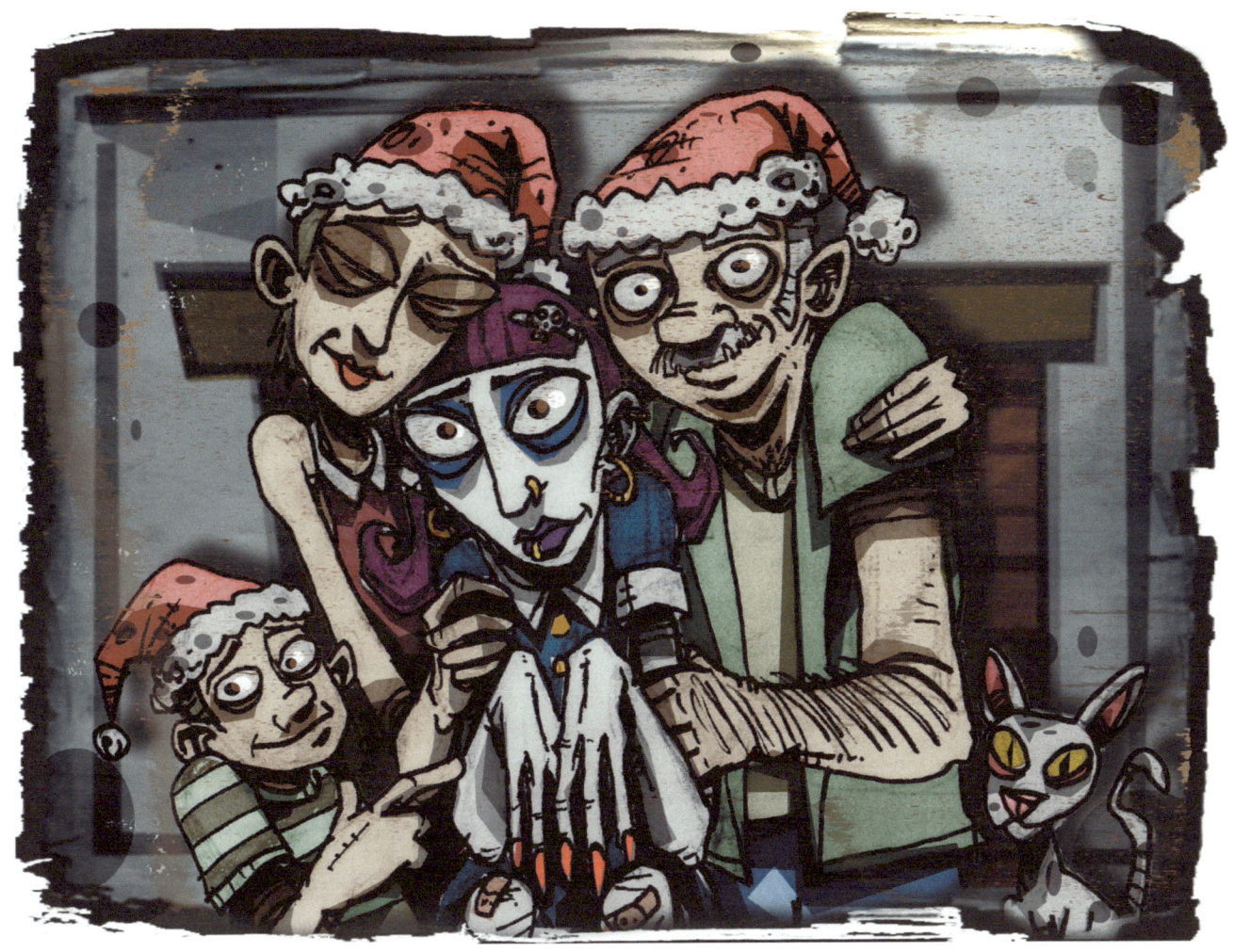

You are an anti-religious agnostic with a taste for esoteric philosophy and mind-altering substances, but your friends and family love you, even if you don't believe in their god.

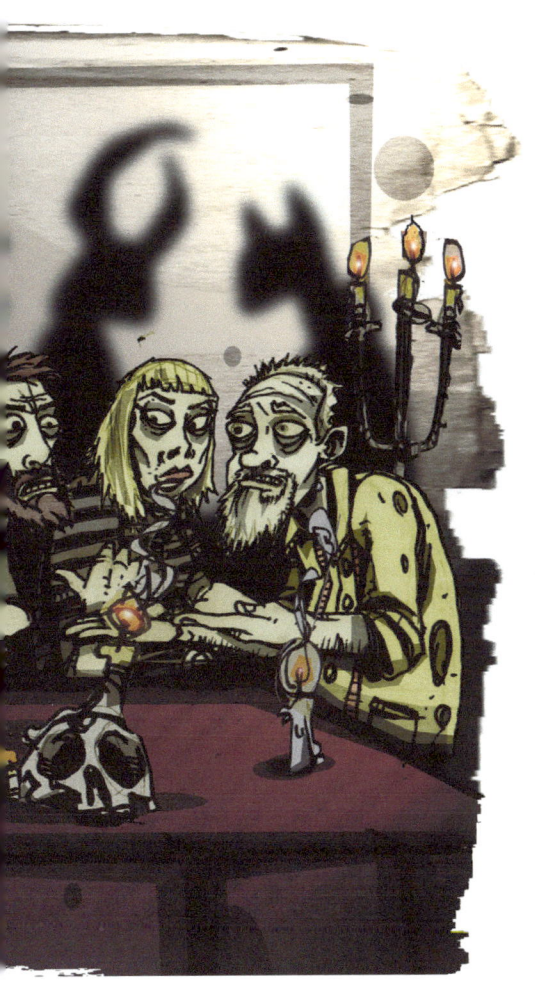

You Might Be a Psychedelic Chaosatanist If....

You think horned gods have been the scapegoats of humanity, denied and condemned, just like our own animal natures. These Theriomorphic archetypes require redemption and conscious reconciliation to heal our divided identities.

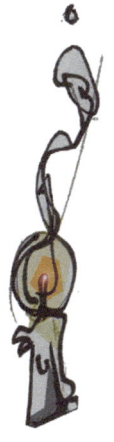

You Might Be a Psychedelic Chaosatanist If....

A couple of hundred years ago, you would have been burned as a witch.

You Might Be a Psychedelic Chaosatanist If....

You got bored of Wicca, exhausted by the elaborations of ceremonial magick, burned-out on Western flavors of Buddhism, turned-off by secret societies and generally over-dosed on post-modern esoteric conjecture, but you still think horned gods are sexy…

you might be a
Psychedelic
CHAO-
SATANIST

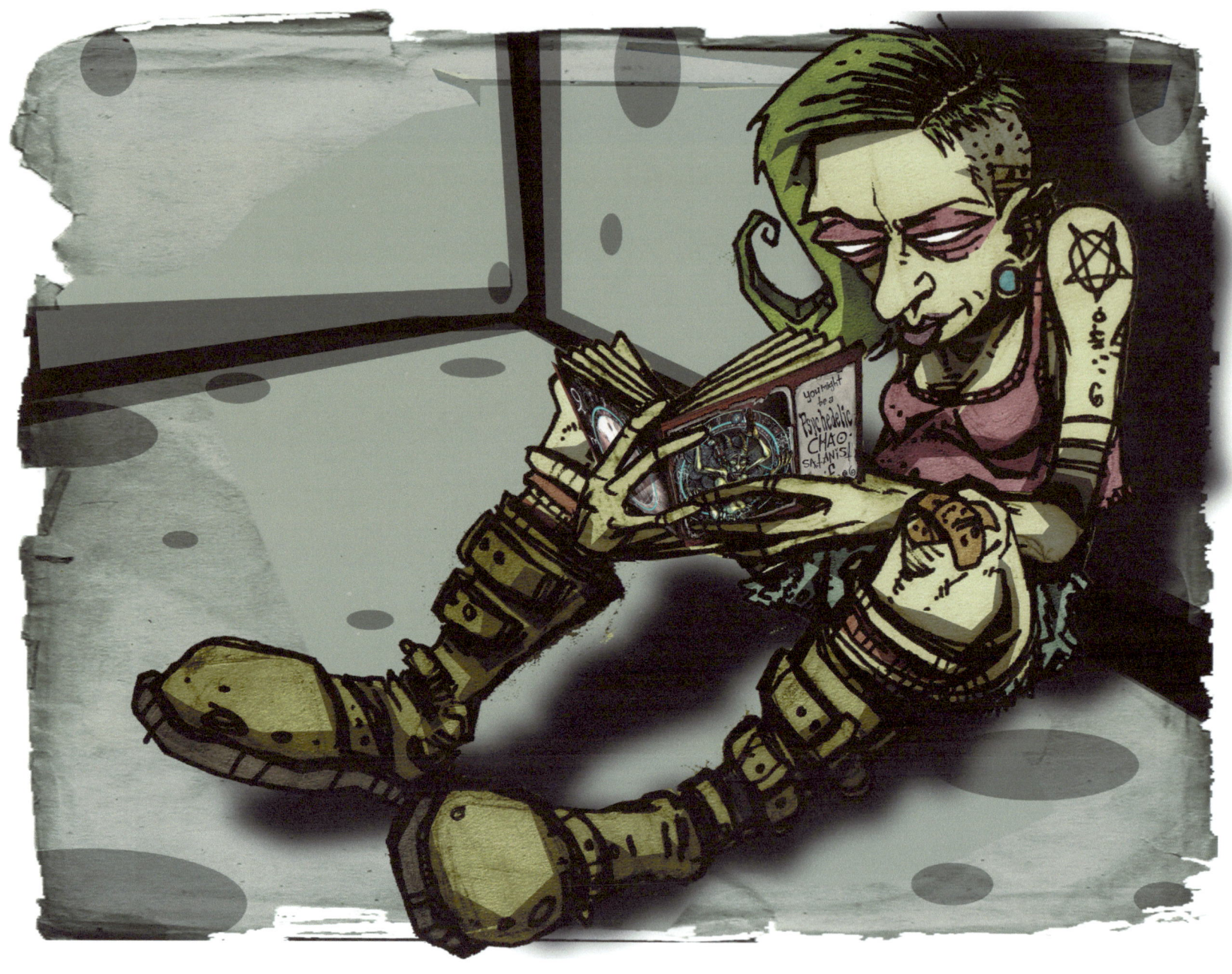

Then, you might be.

www.ingramcontent.com/pod-product-compliance
Lightning Source LLC
Chambersburg PA
CBHW041324290426

44108CB00005B/124